MW01134616

Shaping Worship

70 Devotions for Worship Leaders and Teams

Pastor Steve Baney, M. Div.

Shaping Worship

Published in Bowling Green, Ohio, USA

In 2012

By Steve Baney, M. Div.

Printed in the United States of America
by Lulu.com

ISBN 978-1-300-00956-6

Where To Buy This Book

For more information about buying copies of this book and others like it, please visit

http : // shop . my own little reality . com /

(no spaces)

Table of Contents

Introduction – How To Use This Book

You are a worship leader. Every time we gather for worship, whether you're holding a microphone, playing a keyboard, strumming a guitar, or running a sound system, you are leading others in worship. The example you set can either lead people *toward* worship or *away* from it.

The question isn't *whether* you will lead people; it's *where* you will lead them.

Worship shapes us. It strips away the illusions of this temporary world and focuses our attention back on the eternal. It draws us near to our God where we become aware of our sin, receive God's mercy, and experience cleansing and freedom. Worship influences our thought patterns, speech, attitudes, and behaviors. Our lives are shaped by worship.

As worship leaders, *we shape worship.* We identify songs with lyrics that support the Scripture, that express words that connect with the hearts of God's people. We find biblical texts that support the sermon. We lead others to pray. And we incorporate all kinds of art as an expression of love for our God. Worship leaders shape worship.

Shaping worship works two ways. *We shape it. It shapes us.*

If we are to respond to this opportunity to shape the worship of others, we must be shaped by our God.

There are ten shapes that describe a worship leader - ten words that identify the character God desires in one who leads worship. These shapes include humility, transparency, order, accountability, abiding, example, skill, excellence, team, and submission. Understanding these qualities will help make you a better leader and a better worshipper.

This book is written for worship band leaders and worship choir leaders, to be used along with the band or choir when you meet each week for practice. These worship devotions challenge you to let our God shape you into the kind of leader he desires most. The book you're reading now includes 70 short devotions that you can use as a team or individually. Teams that read and study these materials together, such as choirs or bands, can take turns to read, answer questions, and pray each week. It's an ideal companion for your weekly worship practice.

Spiritual growth happens in a variety of settings – one-on-one, in small groups, and in larger congregations. Your worship band or worship choir is a small group, a context where spiritual formation should happen. Considering the tremendous influence that your team has upon the congregation, be sure to use this small group as an opportunity to promote spiritual growth.

Lord, let this book be a blessing to those who read it. Use your powerful word in their lives and ministries. Unfold your teaching through the Holy Spirit. Apply these truths to their hearts, that they might be the kind of worship leaders you desire for them to be. Make us yours.

Shaping Worship

Humility – Part 1

John 1 describes Jesus in this way:

"He was in the world, and though the world was made through him, *the world did not recognize him*. He came to that which was his own, but his own did not receive him. Yet to all who received him, to those who believed in his name, he gave the right to become children of God - children born not of natural descent, nor of human decision or a husband's will, but born of God" (10-13).

Plain and simple, we don't recognize Jesus. We like to exclude ourselves from the statement that says "the world did not recognize him." We say to ourselves, I recognize him. If he were here today, I would know him. But the truth is, without the Holy Spirit, none of us know what God is like. Without Scripture, we know very little about God. It took powerful revelation for us to even begin to understand him.

When we recognize Jesus for all who he is, then we are ready to worship. We trust in him, knowing he made it possible for us to be a part of God's family. This father-son / father-daughter relationship we have with God has nothing to do with our accomplishments. We are "children born not of… human decision… but born of God."

This is a humbling idea, especially when it comes to leading worship. God chooses us to be a part of his family, not vice versa. God chooses to include us in his work, not vice versa. We are privileged to be in this ministry, not entitled.

We don't worship when it is convenient. We don't perform to make ourselves look good. We come in *response* to God's initiative.

Lord, we respond to you in worship. You revealed your grace, kindness, and your very self to us. Help us to recognize and receive you into our lives. Take away from us any sense of entitlement. Replace it with humility. Make us yours.

Humility – Part 2

Acts 8 tells the story of a man named Simon who tried to trade what he had to offer in order to become a part of a powerful ministry. Listen to his story…

"When Simon saw that the Spirit was given at the laying on of the apostles' hands, he offered them money and said, 'Give me also this ability so that everyone on whom I lay my hands may receive the Holy Spirit.'

"Peter answered: 'May your money perish with you, because you thought you could buy the gift of God with money! *You have no part or share in this ministry, because your heart is not right before God.* Repent of this wickedness and pray to the Lord. Perhaps he will forgive you for having such a thought in your heart'" (18-22).

Peter understood that nothing we have can earn us a place in ministry. Just as Simon's wealth could not buy him such a position, neither can our musical skills, our talent, our popularity, or anything else we have to offer. Peter said Simon would have no part in the ministry because his heart was not right before God. A worshipping heart is what opens the doors of opportunity in this ministry. Our resources and skills are important. But it is our hearts that God seeks.

Lord, it does not matter how long we have been established in a congregation. Nor does it matter how well-known, well-connected, or well-skilled we are. If our hearts are not right before you, we have no right to be apart of your ministry. Keep us humble. Make us yours.

Humility – Part 3

We have been talking about the attitude of worship. John told us how the world did not recognize Christ, yet he chose us and made it possible for us to be children of God. As God's sons and daughters, recognizing Christ prompts us to worship. Acts 8 told us about how a man named Simon tried to earn his way into ministry; but Peter told him that his heart needed to be right with God before he could minister. We know our resources and skills are important. But it is our hearts that God seeks.

This time I thought we could look at a hymn in Scripture, from Philippians 2 to continue learning more about the attitude of worship.

"Your attitude should be the same as that of Christ Jesus: Who, being in very nature God, did not consider equality with God something to be *grasped*, but made himself nothing, taking the very nature of a servant, being made in human likeness. And being found in appearance as a man, he humbled himself and became obedient to death - even death on a cross!" (5-8).

Jesus set an example for us in many ways. He knew he was chosen for a specific ministry. God sent him on a mission to rescue us. In the same way, God has chosen us for a specific ministry, to be lead worshippers. This is both a privilege and a responsibility.

Yet Jesus never let it go to his head. He could have taken advantage of many situations – letting the people make him king, calling angels from heaven to rescue him, or using his power for any number of selfish purposes. But he didn't try to be anyone or anything other than himself.

We should strive to have the same kind of attitude. God wired us for ministry. He put a love for music in our hearts. He helped us develop skills and talents. Like Christ, we need to be just who we are, and be willing to serve.

Lord, please give us the attitude of Christ. Make us nothing. Make us servants – not those who merely pose as servants, but true servants. Humble us as we obey and serve you. Make us yours.

Humility – Part 4

In the last section, we began looking at a hymn in Philippians 2 to identify a few of the characteristics of Christ's attitude.

We identified how Jesus knew he was chosen for a specific ministry, a privilege, and a responsibility. And he never let it go to his head. He didn't take advantage of his power. And he never tried to be anything other than himself.

Let's continue looking at Philippians 2 now.

"Your attitude should be the same as that of Christ Jesus: Who, being in very nature God, did not consider equality with God something to be grasped, but made himself nothing, taking the very nature of a servant, being made in human likeness. And being found in appearance as a man, *he humbled himself* and became obedient to death - even death on a cross!" (5-8)

Jesus humbled himself. It doesn't say he was easily humbled. It says he actively humbled himself. This sounds to me like a conscious choice. It's not easy to be humbled, especially when we are a part of a ministry that takes place in front of other people. It's great to hear affirmation and encouragement from people about our worship ministry. Let it spur us on towards honoring God. As we serve each other and as we serve God's church, just like Jesus, we need to choose humility.

Jesus' service cost him something great. He gave up more than his rights as the Son of God. He gave up his life. We know from the struggle Jesus revealed through his prayer in the garden that facing death was not an easy choice for him. It stressed him out to his limit. He didn't want to endure torture and murder. But he chose to serve God, even when it cost him.

Lord, shape our hearts and attitudes to be like Christ. Engage us in actively humbling ourselves, especially as we are placed before the eyes and attention of others. Strengthen our commitment as your servants, even when it costs us. Make us yours.

Humility – Part 5

Sometimes being a part of ministry costs us. It costs us convenience. It costs our rights, our time, our energy. But we do it to serve others, to honor God, and to help his congregation.

Paul gave up his home, much of his income, and many of the things he owned in order to travel around telling people about salvation. He wrote about giving up some of his rights for that ministry in 1 Corinthians 9:

"If others have this right of support from you, shouldn't we have it all the more? But we did not use this right. On the contrary, we put up with anything rather than hinder the gospel of Christ" (9:12).

I want to commend you for your sacrifice and selflessness. I want to thank you for your commitment over inconvenience. And I want to praise you for the ways you put the ministry of the gospel ahead of your rights.

Lord, we are willing to serve you and your church, even when it costs us. We give to you our time, our energy, our convenience, and our rights. We are humbled to be your servants. Whatever it takes to support the gospel of Christ, take us and use us in the way you choose. Make us yours.

Humility – Part 6

Let's remember God's generosity. Paul wrote to Titus, a fellow pastor, and encouraged him to stress the importance of remembering God's generosity to us. When we trust God, devote ourselves to doing what is good, and remember his generosity, we end up with what the Scripture calls an excellent profit.

Read this Scripture, and identify God's generosity mentioned here:

"When the kindness and love of God our Savior appeared, he saved us, not because of righteous things we had done, but because of his mercy. He saved us through the washing of rebirth and renewal by the Holy Spirit, whom he poured out on us generously through Jesus Christ our Savior, so that, having been justified by his grace, we might become heirs having the hope of eternal life. This is a trustworthy saying. And I want you to stress these things, so that those who have trusted in God may be careful to devote themselves to doing what is good. These things are excellent and profitable for everyone" (Titus 3.4-8).

Let's identify his generosity as mentioned in this text together.

- His mercy cuts us a break even though we deserve the punishment and consequences of our sin.
- He washes us clean, so we aren't living with the stains of our sin.

- Although our sin caused death in us, we are reborn as new people.

- When we are tired and weary, God's Spirit gives us renewal.

- God generously poured out his Spirit on us, our source of life, peace, and hope.

- His grace to us justifies us, making our record as if we never did anything wrong.

- We are made heirs – those who receive inheritance from the King of the Universe.

Lord God, we recognize your great generosity to us. We know that we are not entitled to be your sons or daughters. Yet you made us family and invited us to be a part of your work here in your church. So we thank you for this privilege of singing, playing music, and worshipping in your church. We humbly offer our skills to you, that they might not honor us, but honor you alone. We give to you our worship, everything that we have, everything that we are. We are yours.

Humility – part 7

What makes a great worship leader? Anybody can stand before others and make an attempt to sing a song. So how do we measure greatness when it comes to leading worship? What would you say?

- Playing with skill
- Choosing the best music
- Singing on pitch
- Reading certain Scriptures
- Enunciating with clarity
- Leading prayer
- Picking a key in comfortable range
- Including elements such as drama
- Something else?

Certainly these ideas above are good things for a worship leader to do. Combining them may make you seem like a great leader. But remember, these are just our ideas. The best way to measure the greatness of one who leads others to worship our God is… God. He sets the criteria. So let's look at what Jesus had to say about greatness:

"At that time, the disciples came to Jesus and asked, 'Who is the greatest in the kingdom of heaven?' He called a little child and had him stand among them. And he said: 'I tell you the truth, unless you change and become like little children, you will never enter the kingdom of heaven. Therefore, *whoever humbles himself like this child is the greatest* in the kingdom of heaven.'" (Matthew 18:1-4 NIV).

Greatness is found in being a humble servant of our God. It doesn't mean we should set the kids loose on stage, banging on the drums, and breaking guitar strings. But it does mean we should think no more of ourselves as musicians, choir members, or leaders than we think of a musically-unlearned child. Humility is the beginning of greatness.

Notice the first thing Jesus told his disciples to do. He grabbed a kid, put him in front of them, and said to his followers, "Unless you change…" To be a great worship leader, you must be humble. To be humble, you must be willing to change. You must recognize that all your years of experience, all the shows you've played, all the scales you've mastered – all of the things that make you think you're great – add up to a very small beginning of what Jesus says will make you a great worship leader.

Your experience isn't bad. Your skills aren't a problem, necessarily. The problem comes when we combine our experience and skills with an attitude that says, "I'm great. My way is the best way. I don't need to change."

Lord, use our experience and our skills as worship leaders. Strip away from us arrogance, ego, and pride. Help us understand that having this greatly important job as leaders of worship is not what makes us great. Fill us with greatness by humbling our hearts. Make us yours.

Transparency – Part 1

Our goal is to reveal Christ, to make him be seen, not ourselves. Because we have skills that enable us to make music that other people enjoy, it is tempting to let such recognition go to our heads. We like being appreciated. We like being praised. We like being recognized as a positive contribution to congregational worship.

John had a peculiar relationship to Jesus. His job was to announce Christ's coming and point the way to him. People became very excited about this news from John. Many took interest in John and even mistakenly wondered if he was the Messiah.

John 3 tells us,
To this John replied, "A man can receive only what is given him from heaven. You yourselves can testify that I said, 'I am not the Christ but am sent ahead of him.' The bride belongs to the bridegroom. The friend who attends the bridegroom waits and listens for him, and is full of joy when he hears the

bridegroom's voice. That joy is mine, and it is now complete. He must become greater; I must become less" (27-30).

In this text, the church is compared to a bride, preparing for her wedding. As leaders in the church, our temptation may be to take the focus from Jesus, the groom, and steal the bride away for ourselves. This would make us no "friend of the bridegroom." We must temper our craving to be recognized and enjoyed by the bride, the church. We must remember that God always see us. Since we play for him, this is all the recognition we should seek. Our responsibility is to keep the bride, the church, safe from any who would steal her away from the groom, Christ – even if that means keeping her safe from ourselves!

Lord, don't ever let us come between you and your church. The church belongs to you, like a bride to her husband. Help us understand our role as a friend of the groom, your friend, and the ones who protect and lead your church. Take everything we do in ministry, and help people see through us as they focus on you. Make us a transparent worship leader. Make us yours.

Transparency – Part 2

What do the following have in common? Jewelry, Shouting Children, and Trendy Clothes. You may be having flashbacks from a recent shopping trip. But that's not my point. These four things are all ways people try to get attention from others.

We like getting attention because it makes us feel good, valued, and important. "Look at me!" a child shouts. She wants her mom's attention. A report is shared about a student's poor behavior. He wants the world to notice him. Even as adults, we show up early, say the right worlds, wear the right clothes, and do everything we can to position ourselves so that the right person will pay attention to us.

We all want someone's attention. Maybe it's a spouse (or that special someone), a boss, a friend, a co-worker. Or maybe somehow we hope to be noticed by God. Yet being seen or recognized should not be our ultimate goal. God always sees you. He knew you before you were born. And his heart is deeply in love with you.

Shaping Worship

Jesus encouraged us when we pray that we can avoid showing off (like some people do) by talking with God is a more private location. "Then your Father, who sees what is done in secret, will reward you" (Matthew 6). Some secrets aren't so bad.

If I was a king coming to announce my entrance into the world, I'd do something like the Count of Monte Cristo – fireworks, a hot air balloon, hand-painted invitations, drinks and dinner at a black tie affair. But the King above all kings, the one who we call the King of the Universe, showed up in a rather unusual way. He didn't descend from on high in a cloud of blazing glory; he showed up in a place where the only room leftover for him was filled with stinky, dirty animals. The political leaders and wealthy dignitaries didn't receive hand-made invitations. In fact, very few people knew this guy was royalty, even when he grew up. There was no feast, no special birthday attire, and no parade. This king made a secret entrance.

But some saw angles in the sky. Wise men saw a special star. And if King Jesus has your attention, then the things of earth will grow strangely dim in the light of his glory and grace. Come, worship the king with me.

Lord, focus our attention on you as we strive to focus the attention of others on you as well. We know you see the things we do in secret (good and bad). You've captured our attention. Please help people see through us, to see you, as we lead worship. Make us yours.

Transparency – part 3

It is a difficult tension for leaders to influence others without grabbing a spotlight for themselves. What some don't realize is that a leader is far more often *put on the spot* than they are *put in the spotlight.*

Listen to Paul's words about transparency in ministry: "We do not preach ourselves, but Jesus Christ as Lord, and ourselves as your servants for Jesus' sake. For God, who said, 'Let light shine out of darkness,' made his light shine in our hearts to give us the light of the knowledge of the glory of God in the face of Christ" (2 Corinthians 4:5-6).

Our goal as leaders in worship is to point people toward God (not to point them toward us). But sometimes our efforts get confused for an attempt to gain personal attention. When God captures our hearts we sing loud and clear. But then people start to wonder why we're singing.

And if we're honest, we'll have to admit that there are times when we do want our efforts to gain attention. This is what

Paul calls "preaching ourselves as Lord." Preaching involves communication in an attempt to sway someone's opinion or behavior. To preach myself as Lord means I'm making an effort to get others to look up to me and/or follow me in unhealthy ways. They're looking for an amazing Messiah? Well, wait until they see the dazzling show I have in store for them! This is obviously not the attitude of a worship leader.

Look at the antidote. Paul said Jesus is Lord and we are your servants for his sake. The opposite of preaching ourselves is service. Sin causes darkness to grow in us. When our sin is forgiven and cleansed, there is the natural temptation to feel better about ourselves than we ought. But who is it that brought the light to replace the darkness in our sinful hearts? God made his light shine in our hearts.

When we do a good job, and people compliment us, should we say, "I stink!" and reject their praise? No, that's the kind of false humility that seeks more compliments. A transparent servant doesn't deny his or her strengths or accomplishments. Instead they recognize where their strengths came from. They're honest about their weaknesses. And they choose to intentionally point people's attention to our God.

Lord, whether we're on stage or in our secret place, you see everything we do. We commit to intentionally pointing people's attention to you, even if it costs us. Help us reveal your glory so people can see how amazing you truly are.

We don't want to preach ourselves, to promote ourselves, or prove our own worth. We want to preach, promote, and prove you instead. We are yours.

Transparency – part 4

Sometimes at the end of a well-crafted sermon full of vivid illustrations and emotional depth, there is no response from those who heard it. Despite how well planned the sermon may have been, people don't always respond. How can such wise and persuasive words have no effect on the hearts of the listener? It might be because there is more to preaching than words.

In the same way, there is more to leading worship than playing an instrument or singing a lyric. Read what Paul said regarding effective preaching, and apply it to leading worship:

"My message and my preaching were not with wise and persuasive words, but with a demonstration of the Spirit's power, so that your faith might not rest on men's wisdom, but on God's power" (1 Corinthians 2:4-5).

Shaping Worship

When the power of the Holy Spirit was shown as the source of Paul's preaching, hearts were touched, souls were saved, and lives were changed forever. Certainly there have been preachers along the years whose words were both wise and persuasive. But it is God's Spirit who makes the message take effect.

In the same way, you can study music theory, memorize scales, mimic famous musicians, even play the top-ten songs. But if you hope for your ministry of leading worship to have any substance or power, it must find its source in the Spirit of God.

Be sure to notice the reason Paul stated for his source being the Spirit instead of human skill: so that your faith might not rest on men's wisdom, but on God's power.

Yes, you have wisdom and skill. Otherwise you would probably not be chosen as a leader. But don't rely solely on these human strengths. Remember this: the test of your worship ministry will not be measured by your success, but by your failures. When your human strength fails, if God's powerful Spirit is still demonstrated, then you can call your ministry a success.

Lord, give me strength beyond myself, even if it means taking my strength away. Make me skillful in your ways, even if it means losing my human skill. Establish your wisdom in my heart, and replace what I thought used to be so wise so that when others look at me, they can see past my human weakness and notice you instead. Make us yours.

Transparency – Part 5

Do your neighbors know that you're a follower of Jesus Christ? Do your co-workers? How might they be able to tell?

For some, we can tell by the way they face difficulty. Perhaps there is an illness or financial hardship. Yet they continue to trust in God's care and provision. A supernatural strength surrounds them as they face troubles of many kinds.

For others, we can tell by their sense of clear direction from God, the success of their decisions, their deep understanding of spiritual things. The presence of God is evident in their life. Just being near them makes others feel somehow different, lifted, encouraged, or even blessed.

Still others show their faith in Christ through their strong commitment to living a holy life, investment into God's kingdom, and trusting in the word of God. They have evaluated the options for religion, philosophy, and life; and now they cannot be swayed away from their strong commitment.

Shaping Worship

Scripture describes this kind of evidence of faith in Christ:

"Our gospel came to you not simply with words, but also with power, with the Holy Spirit and with deep conviction. You know how we lived among you for your sake" (1 Thessalonians 1:4-5).

Words are helpful in communicating information about the good news of salvation through faith in Christ. Yet a living testimony filled with power, the Spirit of God, and deep conviction carries the potential to transform lives.

So ask yourself: how might others be able to tell that I am a follower of Jesus Christ? What irrefutable evidence do I show them? How do I face difficulty and hardship? How is my trust in God shown by my attitudes and actions? Where is the Holy Spirit most active in my life? Do I truly have a deep conviction for Christ? Am I fully committed to holy living, investing in God's kingdom, and trusting in his word?

Lord, shine through us so that others might see you, alive and active in our hearts and lives. Inspire our words. Fill us with your power. Shape us and lead us by your Spirit. And deepen our conviction and commitment to Jesus Christ, our Lord. Make us yours.

Transparency – Part 6

Have you ever heard of Bezalel and Oholiab?

These two famous people are mentioned over and over in the end of the book of Exodus. So why don't many of us know them? If you don't believe they are famous, consider their well-known accomplishments listed in Exodus 31:

- They were chosen by God (v 2).
- They were filled with the Holy Spirit, given divine wisdom, understanding, knowledge and all kinds of skills (v 3)
- They designed and created art of gold, silver, bronze, stone, and wood (v 4-5)
- Their art was central in the Tent of Meeting, the Ark of the Covenant (and its atonement cover) (v 7)
- They made the pieces of furniture in the tent like tables, lamp stands, the incense altar, the burnt offering altar, the utensils, the water basin, and the woven garments worn by the priests (v 7-11)

We don't know their *names*. But we certainly recognize the importance of their creative *ministry* in worship.

This is the same kind of reputation we should seek to have as worship leaders. We don't want people to focus on us, who we are, our names, our personality, etc. Instead, we want to be so transparent in the way we point others to worship God that all they remember is *him*. We want people to focus on God, who God is, his name, his personality, and more.

Lord, make us transparent worship leaders, just like Bezalel and Oholiab. Let people forget about us but remember you. Let our contributions to worship help others to draw near to you (not to us). We are yours.

Transparency - Part 7

After Jesus' death and resurrection, he appeared to many people. But some of us didn't recognize him. After all, who would expect that he could conquer death?

You might enjoy reading the story of two people who met Jesus along the road to Emmaus in Luke 24. They didn't realize that the man they met was Jesus Christ (until later)! Here's a short line taken from that story:

"Then the two from Emmaus told their story of how Jesus had appeared to them as they were walking along the road, and how they had recognized him as he was breaking the bread" (Luke 24:35).

They had walked and talked together for a long time. And the topic of their conversation was Jesus' life, ministry, and death. Then they finally recognized Jesus when he did something that they had previously done together - he ate with them.

Like this story, our goal as worship leaders should be to

- walk with people
- talk with them about Jesus
- do the things that Jesus did/does so that others can recognize him in us

What do you think it looks like to do these three things in your life and ministry? Be specific.

Lord, shine through our lives and ministry with such transparency that people will immediately recognize you, your life within us, and your ministry through us. We are yours.

Order – Part 1

You've probably been at a worship gathering (attending or leading) when things obviously did not go as planned. Many factors contribute to how well worship happens, some that are beyond our control. When plans change, it can be wonderful (if it is directed by God) or terrible (if it is directed by our neglect to plan appropriately). In order to give our best to God, we open ourselves to the leading of his Spirit and carefully plan an experience and environment to encourage people to encounter God. This kind of preparation is, in itself, a form of worship.

Paul's letter to the church in Corinth talks about our preparation for worship, specifically including how important he believed spiritual gifts to be as a part of worship. When the people of the church gather together, they bring with them a unique mix of the passions, skills, experiences, personalities, and gifts that God has given them. This can be a recipe for something wonderful, or a formula for disaster. Our differences can be a collage, or a hodgepodge of messy clutter. This makes the proper understanding and use of our spiritual gifts an important prerequisite to worship.

Shaping Worship

Paul wrote: "Therefore, my brothers, be eager to prophesy, and do not forbid speaking in tongues. But everything should be done in a fitting and orderly way" (14:39-40).

Let's offer fitting, orderly worship to our God by being punctual, professional, and prepared.

Lord, we give to you our time. Knowing that many responsibilities in our schedule pull us in multiple directions, using our time and energy, we commit to offer you this time of preparation for worship. We give to you our best because you deserve it. So we commit to be the best we can be, as professional as possible, by focusing our skills in practice. And we give to you this time of preparation. Use it to shape our competence with our instruments and voices, our hearts with great passion for you, and our minds, for we are wholly yours.

Order – Part 2

Genesis 1:1-2 says, "In the beginning God created the heavens and the earth. Now the earth was formless and empty, darkness was over the surface of the deep, and the Spirit of God was hovering over the waters."

The text goes on to describe how there was no light, no distinction between the sky and the earth, no dry ground, no plant life, no sun, moon, or stars, no fish or birds, no animals, and no people. It was a crazy, chaotic place!

The creation account in Genesis details how God brought order and beauty to things that were formless and chaotic. We see throughout Scripture that he is a God of order, not confusion. As imitators of our God, those who worship him should seek to live by the same order and beauty.

How do you think we can show signs of honoring God's order as worship leaders?

- Punctuality
- Professionalism
- Accountability
- Dependability
- Flexibility
- Other: _____

Lord, you are a God of order and beauty. Help us to lead worship in an orderly and beautiful way. Help us to be prepared. Make us ready to serve you and your church. We commit to being the best worship leaders we can be. Help us combine flexibility with dependability, so that when others come to worship, they can know we have prepared specifically for them to worship. Make us yours.

Order – Part 3

Let's read John 6:5-15.

"When Jesus looked up and saw a great crowd coming toward him, he said to Philip, 'Where shall we buy bread for these people to eat?' He asked this only to test him, for he already had in mind what he was going to do.

"Philip answered him, 'Eight months' wages would not buy enough bread for each one to have a bite!'

"Another of his disciples, Andrew, Simon Peter's brother, spoke up, 'Here is a boy with five small barley loaves and two small fish, but how far will they go among so many?'

"Jesus said, 'Have the people sit down.' There was plenty of grass in that place, and the men sat down, about five thousand of them. Jesus then took the loaves, gave thanks, and distributed to those who were seated as much as they wanted. He did the same with the fish.

"When they had all had enough to eat, he said to his disciples, 'Gather the pieces that are left over. Let nothing be wasted.' So they gathered them and filled twelve baskets with the pieces of the five barley loaves left over by those who had eaten.

"After the people saw the miraculous sign that Jesus did, they began to say, 'Surely this is the Prophet who is to come into the world.' Jesus, knowing that they intended to come and make him king by force, withdrew again to a mountain by himself."

The need for food was greater than what the disciples were able or ready to provide. It would take eight months worth of a person's income in order to feed a crowd this large. Even if they could afford it, it didn't seem wise. But God made a provision. Andrew saw a boy who was willing to share his food (or Andrew was bigger than the unwilling kid). When Jesus used what God had provided, he did not do so haphazardly.

Don't waste what God provides! Jesus instructed them to get the leftovers so nothing would be wasted.

When the people saw this great miracle they responded in worship. You may not think of it as worship, but it was! They didn't pull out hymnals and choir robes (although they could have). They worshiped Jesus with words of praise. *This guy is the prophet we've been looking for. He's here to speak God's message to us.*

Shaping Worship

This is the Messiah, here to save us from all evil. When God provides for our needs, our natural response should be worship.

One more important note on the last verse: Was Jesus rightfully a king? Yes, of course, he is the King of kings. So would it have been a good thing for these people to crown him as their king, to worship and serve him with their lives? Maybe, maybe not. We often want good things. Worshipping and serving Jesus as king is a good thing. We often plan things that are right. They planned to make Jesus their rightful king. But God had a better plan that involved Jesus' self-sacrifice to pay the penalty for sin. Jesus knew it was not the right time for him to be crowned as the king of these people. Plan good things. Plan right things. But always remember God's plan, God's order may be different – better – than ours.

Lord, we recognize your provision and turn to you with gratitude in our hearts. Let our blessings reminds us of the ways you invite us to participate in your ministry to provide for the needs of others. Let us be wise in the way we use what you provide - our skills, time, energy, attention, and passion. Let your provision and ministry lead people to worship you. And in all this, help us to remember that as we plan good and right things, you plan and your order may be different – better – than ours. Make us yours.

Order – Part 4

Think of how a mother or father would feel upon realization that they had accidentally left their child alone in a store after shopping. Frantically, the parents rush back to look for the child. Questions of the child's safety race through their minds. What if something terrible has happened? This may have been similar to the way Jesus' parents felt in Luke 2.

"Every year his [Jesus'] parents went to Jerusalem for the Feast of the Passover. When he was twelve years old, they went up to the Feast, according to the custom. After the Feast was over, while his parents were returning home, the boy Jesus stayed behind in Jerusalem, but they were unaware of it. Thinking he was in their company, they traveled on for a day. Then they began looking for him among their relatives and friends. When they did not find him, they went back to Jerusalem to look for him. After three days they found him in the temple courts, sitting among the teachers, listening to them and asking them questions. Everyone who heard him was amazed at his understanding and his answers. When his parents saw him, they were astonished. His mother said to him, 'Son, why have you treated us like this? Your father and I have been anxiously searching for you'" (41-48).

This is how the worship leader feels when the drummer doesn't show up, or when the sound technician is absent, or when the keyboardist has gone missing. Questions of their well-being race through the worship leader's mind. In addition to concern for the missing team member, the worship leader also begins to worry about what kind of effect this will have upon the congregation. Can the band play that upbeat song without the drummer? Will anyone be able to hear the choir without the sound technician controlling the microphones? What will the band do when the pianist's lead solo goes missing from the instrumental portion of that song?

Your ministry of worship is important. When you are missing, there is a void left behind. If you need time off for vacation, illness, or other responsibilities, your worship leader understands these needs. And he or she will work with you to arrange for the time off that you need. But the only excuse for your absence without a phone call is an emergency. When you skip practice or worship without telling the worship leader where you are, he or she comes to one of two conclusions.

(1)   There is some sort of emergency. Because they care about you (as a person, not just as a function of the

band), they will want to know how they can help respond to the emergency. Or…

(2)   You don't respect the leader, the band, the congregation, or our God enough to let the worship leader know where you are and why you're absent.

Since we worship a God of order - not a God of chaos or confusion – let's agree to be on time for practice and worship. Let's be dependable - the team member that others can always count on to show up. And let's worship God in an orderly way, prioritizing his team and his congregation over our personal desires.

Lord, we will worship you with order. We commit to being on time and present at practice and at worship. And when we cannot be present or on time, we commit to respecting your team, your congregation, and the worship leader you placed over us by letting he or she know where we are and why we're absent or late. Take our time and make it yours. Make us yours.

Order - Part 5

The first letter to the Corinthian Church speaks much about worship. Chapter 14 describes how prophecy can build up the church when done in a godly way. It also describes how various aspects of corporate worship (such as prayer and speaking in other languages) are only helpful when they make sense to the others who are there.

Yes, God understands the worship in our hearts, even when its expression might seem strange to other people. Yet *our job as worship leaders goes far beyond expressing what is in our hearts*. It involves expressing our worship to God in ways that edify other people in our presence. (To edify means to build up).

"If you are praising God with your spirit [in an unknown language], how can one who finds himself among those who do not understand say 'Amen' to your thanksgiving, since he does not know what you are saying? You may be giving thanks well enough, but the other man is not edified" (1 Corinthians 14:16-17).

Our worship should always be sincere. And when we are leading others in worship, we must always remember what kinds of worship languages they understand and speak. For example, an elderly woman might find it much easier and edifying to worship by using traditional hymns rather than the newest rap or rock and roll. Praise God from whom all blessings flow, dawg!

Lord, as we lead worship, help us to express our worship in ways that edify (build up) others. And when we worship alone, that will be our chance to use the expressions that are truest to our hearts' native tongue. Use us as worship leaders who consider the edification of others before our own. Make us yours.

Order - Part 6

Have you ever planned a big party? You need food, decorations, music, invitations, games, and more. It seems that the bigger the party is, the more complicated the planning becomes.

The same can be true of congregational worship. When we gather to worship our God, in some ways it's like throwing a big party. It might involve communion, decor, music, handouts, video projection, and more.

Because Paul understood the importance of careful planning for congregational worship, he wrote about it in Scripture. Let's look at some select lines from 1 Corinthians 14 together.

"When you come together, everyone has a hymn, or a word of instruction, a revelation, a tongue or an interpretation. All of these must be done for the strengthening of the church. If anyone speaks in a tongue, two - or at the most three - should speak, one at a time, and someone must interpret" (26-27).

These first few lines introduce the complexities of various elements in worship - music, teaching, and prayer. Notice the purpose of these worship elements listed in verse 26: *to strengthen the church.*

"Two or three prophets should speak, and the others should weigh carefully what is said. And if a revelation comes to someone who is sitting down, the first speaker should stop. For you can all prophesy in turn so that everyone may be instructed and encouraged" (29-31).

For our purposes, focus less here on the topic of prophecy and more on the *procedure* that Paul prescribes in verse 31. Many people come together to do their thing. It's like he's saying, "You can all [do your part in leading worship] in turn so that everyone may be [blessed by your ministry]."

"God is not a God of disorder but of peace... Everything should be done in a fitting and orderly way" (33, 40).

What is absent when our worship is disorderly? The peace of God.

Lord, help us to lead worship in a fitting and orderly way. Let your Holy Spirit guide us as we carefully plan. Tune our hearts to your desire as we lead, showing us the direction you want our worship to go. Make us yours.

Order – Part 7

If God can only lead us when we're "winging it" - making things up as we go without preparation - then we would be serving a very weak God. Yes, we need to be sensitive to the times when God wants us to change our plans. But this does not mean we stop planning altogether. Jesus spoke about the value and benefits of those who prepared for celebrating with him.

"The kingdom of heaven will be like ten virgins who took their lamps and went out to meet the bridegroom. Five of them were foolish and five were wise. The foolish ones took their lamps but did not take any oil with them. The wise, however, took oil in jars along with their lamps.

"The bridegroom was a long time in coming, and they all became drowsy and fell asleep. At midnight the cry rang out: 'Here's the bridegroom! Come out to meet him!'

"Then all the virgins woke up and trimmed their lamps. The foolish ones said to the wise, 'Give us some of your oil; our lamps are going out.'

"'No,' they replied, 'there may not be enough for both us and you. Instead, go to those who sell oil and buy some for yourselves.'

"But while they were on their way to buy the oil, the bridegroom arrived. The virgins who were ready went in with him to the wedding banquet. And the door was shut.

"Later the others also came. 'Sir! Sir!' they said. 'Open the door for us!'

"But he replied, 'I tell you the truth, I don't know you'" (Matthew 25:1-12).

This story describes two kinds of people: those who prepare and those who do not. The wise virgins who prepared in advance were invited into the celebration and got to enjoy the party with the groom. But Jesus described those who did not adequately prepare as foolish. They were not invited into the celebration. They did not get to know the groom (*I do not know you*).

Lord, help us to plan carefully so we will be ready to celebrate with you. Make us wise in our preparation. Make us ready when your Spirit calls, "Here's the bridegroom! Come out to meet him!" Let us know you more as we celebrate in worship. Make us yours.

Accountability – Part 1

God's prophets were the ones he chose to deliver his messages, teach his people, and set the example to follow. As a worship leader, you are a like those prophets, chosen by God to share a message and lead God's people. As a minister and a leader, you are responsible for others. People will learn about worship and about how to worship from you. Do you think your example of worship is worthy of being duplicated by others in the church? You will be held accountable for your example.

Look at the responsibility God gave his prophet Ezekiel… "Son of man, I have made you a watchman for the house of Israel; so hear the word I speak and give them warning from me. When I say to the wicked, 'O wicked man, you will surely die,' and you do not speak out to dissuade him from his ways, that wicked man will die for his sin, and *I will hold you accountable* for his blood. But if you do warn the wicked man to turn from his ways and he does not do so, he will die for his sin, but you will have saved yourself" (Ezekiel 33:7-9).

If we lead people away from God by the things we say or the things we do, we are responsible for their sin. But if we lead people to Jesus, we'll get to share in the celebration, as we all worship the same Lord.

Lord, help us to understand this great responsibility you've given us as worship leaders. Open our eyes to what your people are doing, not so we can look down and judge them, but so we can be careful to lead them to you. Make us aware of our responsibility as leaders. And hold us accountable as you shape us into the kinds of leaders you desire for us to be. We are yours.

Accountability – Part 2

1 Chronicles 29 describes the resources people pooled together in order to build the Temple. It was a huge undertaking because this wasn't just any old building. This was the house of our Lord. It says King David placed all of his resources at the disposal of this project – gold, silver, bronze, iron, wood, and precious stones.

After showing the extent of his willingness to give, he asked the people an interesting question: "Who is willing to consecrate himself today to the Lord?" (v 5).

When I read this, I was surprised that he didn't ask them *what* they would give. He asked *who was willing to be given*. King David did not ask for a material response. He asked for an offering of the heart, the surrender of oneself in consecration to our Lord. "Who is willing to consecrate himself today to the Lord?"

The leaders of the families, tribes, and armies all responded by giving the same way David did. When the people saw their leaders giving their resources and their lives to the Lord, everybody rejoiced. "Who is willing to consecrate himself today to the Lord?"

Then David prayed, declaring God's power and splendor. Yet he did not submit to self-congratulations. The size of their offering would not measure their devotion to God. If the Temple was filled with gold and precious stones yet their hearts remained unfaithful to God, then the offering to God would be empty. David praised God for the generosity of the people as they gave their resources *and* their hearts.

"Everything comes from you, and we have given you only what comes from your hand… O Lord our God, as for all this abundance that we have provided for building you a temple for your Holy Name, it comes from your hand, and all of it belongs to you. I know, my God, that you test the heart and are pleased with integrity. All these things have I given willingly and with honest intent. And now I have seen with joy how willingly your people who are here have given to you. O Lord, God of our fathers Abraham, Isaac and Israel, keep this desire in the hearts of your people forever, and keep their hearts loyal to you" (14, 16-18).

As we come to worship, remember that God is testing our hearts, not our wallets. Let God's Spirit reveal areas of our hearts where we lack integrity. And invite him to fill us with desire and loyalty to our Lord.

Lord, all we have is at your disposal. Take our resources, for they are already yours. Hold us accountable to our commitment to give our lives to you. Test our heart and show us where we lack integrity. And keep us loyal to you forever. We are yours.

Accountability – Part 3

Who is it that knows you better than anyone else? Think of that person who can complete your sentences. Think of the one who knows what you're thinking before you even say it. They could order food for you at a restaurant and you'd be perfectly happy with what they choose for you. They can prescribe just

Shaping Worship

what you'll do in a given situation. And despite your dark side, they love you anyway. They know your hopes, your dreams, your fears, and your frustrations. They might even know your deepest, darkest secrets. Do you have a friend who knows you like this?

Psalm 139 talks about our God's thorough knowledge of who we are. It says he has examined our hearts and knows everything about us (v 1). He sees everything we do and knows everything we think (v 2). He knows wherever we are, wherever we go (v 3). The little white lies, the victories, the corners we cut, our success and our failure… You know that thing you did years ago that you think you got away with? Ya, he knows about that too. He examines our hearts and knows everything about us.

So if this is true – if our God really knows everything about us – then why does the author of this psalm end with these words?

"Search me, O God, and know my heart;
test me and know my anxious thoughts.
Point out anything in me that offends you,
and lead me along the path of everlasting life."

Why ask God to search and test the deepest, most hidden corners of our lives if he already knows everything about us? I believe the answer is found in the last two lines. When God evaluates our hearts, it isn't for *his* benefit. It's for *ours*. He isn't surprised by what he finds when he peeks in unexpected. The desire of the author of this psalm isn't to educate God about his personal secrets. He was inviting God to hold him accountable, to point out what offends God, and to lead him toward life.

Evaluation is difficult and often uncomfortable. But since we are imperfect people, it's a necessary part of being transformed into Christlikeness. Think again of that person who knows you so well. Have you given them permission to hold you accountable, to guard you from sin, to challenge your weakness, and to demand an account?

Lord, use the words of Psalm 139 as an evaluation of our hearts. Help us agree to be held accountable, even though it can be challenging and unpleasant. Give us the strength to take responsibility, and then to grow past our weakness and failure. Search us, know us, and point out what needs to change. Make us yours.

Accountability – Part 4

In music, a team of people working together can accomplish much more than any single person from the team. This is how melody becomes harmony, soloists become quartets, and musicians become orchestras. We are better together.

The same thing is true in life. Alone, we have a tendency to make excuses for our sin, hiding it from others, and acting like it isn't a problem. But when others who love us become aware of our sin, they hold the potential to empower us to overcome it. Scripture even asks us to help each other in this way:

"See to it, brothers and sisters, that none of you has a sinful, unbelieving heart that turns away from the living God. But encourage one another daily, as long as it is called 'Today,' so that none of you may be hardened by sin's deceitfulness" (Hebrews 3:12-13).

For a worship leader and worship band to be successful, the whole team must work together. At times this means helping each other learn rhythm, melody, and lyrics. Other times this means holding each other accountable to the call of Christ to live free from sin.

If you haven't already, consider giving your team permission to hold you accountable. They want to help. Yet they don't want to insult you or overstep their bounds. So tell them it's okay for them to call you out when you mess up. Give them the right to address issues of sin, selfishness, speech, attitude, and action that need to change.

Lord, help us to hold our team accountable. Show us how to speak with love, especially when we need to rebuke. And help us to listen when others hold us accountable, knowing that they love us, and have our best interest and the team's best interest in mind. We are yours.

Accountability – Part 5

What is your natural tendency when you see someone doing something sinful? Do you say something to the person? Do you talk about them to someone else? Or do you ignore it altogether?

In Christian circles, we call this accountability. Accountability does not mean judging others. It does not mean condemnation. It means helping others find strength in your support when they feel weak in the face of temptation.

All too often, we don't talk about sin because we don't want to offend people. The excuse we tell ourselves has something to do with our own sinfulness, suggesting it disqualifies us from helping others deal with their sin. The truth is, we all sin. So when we hold others accountable for their sin, it's not because we're perfect; it's because we love them.

"Brothers and sisters, if someone is caught in a sin, you who live by the Spirit should restore that person gently. But watch yourselves, or you also may be tempted" (Galatians 6:1).

Notice that the Scripture does not say, If someone is caught in sin, make them feel *ashamed, embarrassed, or worthless.* No one likes to be embarrassed. And no one likes to be rebuked. But a true friend gives warning when they see danger.

If you see someone on your team sinning, take responsibility for the team and deal with it gently. Ignoring it will only hurt the team, and ultimately hurt you. Restore them gently. Do it the way you'd like someone to do it to you. And be ready for them to hold you accountable too.

Lord, help us to keep our team accountable. Let us live by the Spirit, restoring each other gently when we sin. Use us to support each other in this way. Make us yours.

Accountability – Part 6

Each person in a team is responsible for all of the other members of the team. Unfortunately, at one time or another, we will all let our team down. Perhaps due to personal life circumstances, or as a result of poor choices – whatever the reason, all of us fail from time to time. And all of us need our team to help us through our tough times and failures. In order to accomplish this kind of integrated team support, ministry teams must maintain accountability.

"Let us consider how we may spur one another on toward love and good deeds, not giving up meeting together, as some are in the habit of doing, but encouraging one another — and all the more as you see the Day approaching" (Hebrews 10:24-25).

Accountability seems to have a pattern. There are seasons when we are up front, honest, even blunt with our accountability partners. Then for multiple reasons, we enter into seasons where we feel reluctant to be forthright. These seasons come naturally and repeatedly. So what can we do about them?

Find a way to spur (poke, prod, encourage, twist one's arm, coax, etc.) one another on. Don't give up. Encourage each other. Love that lasts through failure will keep accountability alive. When was the last time you reminded your teammates that you'll love them even when they fail? These regular reminders will build the team and edify the lives of each team member.

Conversely, when was the last time you gave your team permission to ask you those tough questions? Do they know they're still allowed to ask you to give an account? It will help you and strengthen the team when you do this.

Lord, use us to keep our team accountable. Help us to love them through their difficulties and failures. We will show them the same kind of grace that we need them to show us. Make us accountable to each other, so we can spur each other on toward love and good deeds. We are yours.

Accountability – Part 7

What do the following lines of Scripture have in common?

"Young people, it's wonderful to be young! Enjoy every minute of it. Do everything you want to do; take it all in. But remember that you must give an account to God for everything you do" (Ecclesiastes 11:9).

"A good person produces good things from the treasury of a good heart, and an evil person produces evil things from the treasury of an evil heart. I tell you this, you must give an account on judgment day for every idle word you speak" (Matthew 12:35-36).

"The Scriptures say, 'As surely as I live,' says the Lord, 'every knee will bend to me, and every tongue will confess and give praise to God.' Yes, each of us will give a personal account to God. So let's stop condemning each other. Decide instead to live in such a way that you will not cause another believer to stumble and fall" (Romans 14:11-13).

What do these lines of Scripture have in common? They all address the issue of accountability.

The first line (from Ecclesiastes) says we have the freedom to choose to do anything. But we should remember that we ultimately have to give an account to God. He will hold us responsible for those choices.

The second line (from Matthew) says we will be accountable, not just for our actions, but also for our words. The things we say have a powerful impact on us and those around us. Jesus spoke harshly to religious leaders who hurt others around them by the things they said and did.

The third line (from Romans) includes a quote from Isaiah 49. God ensures that we understand that we are responsible for our choices. This line says we should be more concerned about our own accountability than we are in condemning others.

Lord, help us to understand the importance of accountability as worship leaders. We will take responsibility for the things we say and do. And we will commit to live in such a way that we will not hurt others or ourselves. Make us yours.

Shaping Worship

Abiding – Part 1

Carl Albrecht, professional drummer and worship leader for over 30 years, teaches: "Don't forsake your time with the Lord as you serve the Lord." Why do you think we do this sometimes? Why do we spend more time listening to imperfect people than we do listening to God? What do you suppose happens to the quality of our ministry when we aren't intentionally including God in our daily lives? These are questions that we need to reflect on. Listen to Jesus' words on this subject:

"I am the true vine, and my Father is the gardener. He cuts off every branch in me that bears no fruit, while every branch that does bear fruit he prunes so that it will be even more fruitful. You are already clean because of the word I have spoken to you. *Remain in me, and I will remain in you.* No branch can bear fruit by itself; it must remain in the vine. Neither can you bear fruit unless you remain in me. I am the vine; you are the branches. If a man remains in me and I in him, he will bear much fruit; *apart from me you can do nothing.*" ~ John 15:1-5

Shaping Worship

When Jesus said he is the true vine, it suggests that we sometimes draw nourishment and energy from false vines, those that were not made for us. Think of the ways, places, and people that give you energy, support, and identity. Are these of God?

Jesus mentioned that the fruit-bearing branches get pruned and cleaned up. How did he say this happens? God trims back certain areas of our lives, hacking off others, and cleans us up into healthy, fruit-producing branches by integrating his word into our lives (verse 3).

Jesus' instruction to remain in him (verse 4) would make no sense if we did not have the option (or should I say danger) of ceasing to remain in him. Here is where Jesus points out the real danger of participating in ministry for him while not intentionally drawing our life from him. Simply put: *we cannot bear fruit without him.* The product of our so-called ministry without him is always rotten fruit. "Apart from me," he said, "you can do nothing." Nothing, nada, zilch, zippo, squat!

Ah, but what a different it makes when we stay connected to the true vine, drawing our nourishment from the author of life. "This is to my Father's glory," Jesus continued in verse 8, "that you bear much fruit, showing yourselves to be my disciples."

Lord God, source of life, we turn to you as the one, true vine. We invite you to prune and clean us by making your word – your commands and your desires – the basis for our living. Remind us to always remain in you. Show us when we turn to other false vines – people, experiences, habits, or accomplishments. As we abide deeply in you, grow the fruit of ministry that brings glory to you God, blesses your people, and expands your kingdom now and forever. Make us yours.

Abiding – Part 2

Effective ministry is the result of a quality relationship with God, not vice versa. How do we nurture a relationship like this? Hebrews 10:22-25 says:

Let us *draw near to God* with a sincere heart in full assurance of faith, having our hearts sprinkled to cleanse us from a guilty conscience and having our bodies washed with pure water. Let us hold unswervingly to the hope we profess, for he who promised is faithful. And let us consider how we may spur one another on toward love and good deeds. Let us not give up meeting together, as some are in the habit of doing, but let us encourage one another - and all the more as you see the Day approaching.

In this text I see six things we can do to "draw near to God," nurturing a quality relationship with him…

(1) Be sincere about our relationship with God

(2) Have faith in God (the combination of our trust and obedience)

(3) Be cleansed by God – Let him clean up your life

(4) Hold onto the hope we find in God's Word ("what we profess")

(5) Encourage ("spur") one another to love and good actions

(6) Get together with other Christians

Lord, we aren't perfect. So help us to be sincere as we pursue you. We know we can trust you. So in faith, we will obey. By your Spirit, come and cleanse our hearts. Let your word soak into our lives so that we can have a firm grasp on it. Show us how we might spur others on toward love and good deeds. And use our times with other Christians to shape and encourage us. We are yours.

Abiding – Part 3

What parts of my body are used when I play guitar in worship? Hands, arms, brain, muscles, bones, etc. Think of what would happen to my ability to play guitar if my fingers were cut off from my left hand (the hand that shapes the chords). Simple: I'd lose my ability to play. And what would happen to the severed fingers? They would shrivel and die. 1 Corinthians uses this same metaphor to teaching about the importance of abiding in Christ:

"The body is a unit, though it is made up of many parts; and though all its parts are many, they form one body. So it is with Christ. The eye cannot say to the hand, 'I don't need you!' And the head cannot say to the feet, 'I don't need you!' On the contrary, those parts of the body that seem to be weaker are indispensable, and the parts that we think are less honorable we treat with special honor. And the parts that are unpresentable are treated with special modesty, while our presentable parts need no special treatment. But God has combined the members of the body and has given greater honor to the parts that lacked it, so that *there should be no division* in the body, but that its parts should have equal concern for each other. If one part suffers, every part suffers with it; if one part is honored, every part rejoices with it" (1 Corinthians 12:12, 21-26).

When we attend worship, we do more than fulfill a command of God. When we participate in a small group, we do more than mark our name on an attendance record. When we learn in a class at church, we do more than academic exercise. When we spend time with God in these ways, we are abiding with him and with his body, the church.

When we don't abide with God and his body, we become like severed fingers that shrivel and die. And our absence from the body impacts its ability to fully function, just like missing fingers would prevent me from playing guitar. If we hope for our ministry to be effective at all, it must come as the result of a quality relationship with God through abiding.

Lord, draw us near to you through our personal time with you and through our connection with your body, this church. Use this kind of abiding as a source of life, energy, passion, and purpose in our lives and ministry. We are yours.

Abiding - Part 4

Christ's sacrifice for us on the cross rescued us from sin and death. In his resurrection, we find new life through our faith by his grace. Jesus told us that he came so that we "may have life, and have it to the full" (John 10:10). Would you characterize your spiritual life as truly *full* in every way?

When asked to do some work, we often tend to do as little as possible. If it's writing a one to two page paper, we write one page. If it's doing some of the laundry, we wash one load. If it's anything in life that we can get away with, we look for ways to minimize our workload.

The same dangerous attitude appears when it comes to spiritual life. We trust God, we pray for forgiveness, we have faith in him, and sadly, we hope that moment of decision is enough to squeeze by. Scripture tells us that if you've placed your faith in Christ, he is faithful to forgive you, to wipe your slate clean. But why did Jesus say he came? Was it to give you a second chance to mess up again? No, the author of life came to give you a full life.

This is the invitation given to us in Colossians 2:6-7:

"So then, just as you received Christ Jesus as Lord, continue to live in him, rooted and built up in him, strengthened in the faith as you were taught, and overflowing with thankfulness."

The do-as-little-as-possible attitude is like a mother telling a newborn infant that it has finished everything it needs in life the moment after the child is born. If you've ever seen a newborn infant, you recognize immediately its need to grow, learn, and develop. It could be technically alive while confined to a hospital bed on IVs for its food and water. But it wouldn't truly be living a *full* life.

In the same way, if we don't continue to dig our spiritual roots down into the rich, life-giving soil found in spiritual formation, our faith grows weak, and our overflow dries up. Will you let the fullness of his life grow in you?

Lord, fill us with your life. Make us firmly rooted in you, drawing our nourishment, strength, and very life from you alone. Build our lives into everything you desire. Strengthen our faith as we learn to live in and for you. And let our lives be a sign of your great work, honoring you with all the glory. Make us yours.

Abiding – Part 5

Long distance relationships are difficult. Space and time separate two people, straining their friendship and limiting their interaction.

The same kind of strain and limitation can happen to our relationship with God. If we limit our exposure, our face-to-face time with God per se, then our relationship suffers. This happens when we pray less, read Scripture less, worship less, and seek his presence less.

Think of some ways we can maintain a long distance relationship with another person. Examples include making phone calls, writing letters, occasional visits, etc. Now apply these same activities to our relationship with God. How can we do these things with him?

Jesus talked about the means of maintaining a close relationship with him:

"If you remain in me and my words remain in you, ask whatever you wish, and it will be done for you" (John 15:7).

The Message puts it this way: "Make yourselves at home with me and my words are at home with you." Let's get comfortable. Kick off your shoes. Take off your coat. Stay for a while.

Does the word of God *belong* in your life? Does it *fit in*? Or does it seem out of place compared to the surroundings? When we abide in Christ, live with him, belong in his presence, our behavior, attitude, decisions, demeanor, and total life are transformed into his likeness.

Lord, help us to abide in you. Show us ways to keep your presence at the front of our attention. Fill our minds and hearts with your words. Change our lives so that we belong with you and you belong with us. Make us yours.

Abiding – Part 6

True or false: Christian life cannot take place until after death.

If we're talking about physical death, the answer is *false*. Christ came to bring life to its fullest (John 10:10), restoring the health, relationships, and lives of those he met in ministry.

But if we're talking about metaphorical death, the answer is *true*. Christian life cannot take place until after the death of our sinful life. Baptism has many symbolic references to the death of the old, sinful way of life, and the resurrection of a new person, a new life, and a new creation in Christ.

"Since, then, you have been raised with Christ, set your hearts on things above, where Christ is, seated at the right hand of God. Set your minds on things above, not on earthly things. *For you died, and your life is now hidden with Christ in God.* When Christ, who is your life, appears, then you also will appear with him in glory" (Colossians 3:1-4).

What practical advice does Paul give here to the church in Colossi?

- *Set your hearts on things above* - fall in love with things that are eternal, things that are heavenly, things that are of God. Dream of them. Hope for them. Strive for them. One day, you will get to enjoy them completely.

- *Set your minds of things above* - The things of this world will distract, distort, and disrupt our minds. Instead, we should think, decide, plan, and act based on the things above, not earthly things.

- *Remember that your old life is dead.* It never was really alive in the first place. There should be an ever-increasing difference between the way you live now versus the way you lived before finding new life in Christ.

- *Let Christ be your life.* Let him live in you by doing what he does. Let him speak in you by saying what he says. Let him act in you by deciding what he decides. This will require you to know him thoroughly. Your goal should be to appear so much like Christ that others might mistake you for him.

Lord, help us to abide in you so deeply that you are our very life. Set our hearts and minds on things above, not the things of this world. Put to death our old ways of living. Fill us instead with a new life in you. Use our new lives as a ministry to others, that they might see and desire the same kind of new life for themselves. We are yours.

Abiding – Part 7

When the end of Moses' ministry and life was approaching, Moses shared important lessons about how to live in relationship with God. When he was finishing his last thoughts, he added:

"*Take to heart* all the words of warning I have given you today. Pass them on as a command to your children so they will obey every word of these instructions" (Deuteronomy 32:46).

One important way we can ensure that we are living the kind of lives God desires for us is to take his word to heart.

When we learn the words to a song or a poem, we sometimes say we know the words "by heart." It's a way of describing the effect that memorization has upon our attitudes, decisions, and lives. Memorizing God's word has an even greater impact on us when we store it in our hearts.

Psalm 119:11 says, "I have hidden your word *in my heart*, that I might not sin against you."

Do you see the potential of memorizing God's word? It can keep us from sin. If you want to enjoy the freedom and blessings associated with the full life that God has designed for you, start by memorizing his words and putting them into action in your life.

Lord, help us to take to heart all of your word. Store it in our hearts, that it might protect us from sin. Help us to abide in you, as your word abides in us. Make us yours.

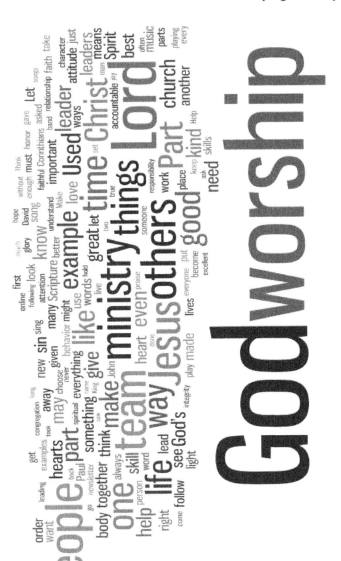

Shaping Worship

Example – Part 1

People will look to us as an example. So we need to be a good example, not a bad one! We are held responsible for the way we lead others. Let's lead them to Jesus.

"We, who with unveiled faces all *reflect* the Lord's glory, are being transformed into *his likeness* with ever-increasing glory, which comes from the Lord, who is the Spirit. Therefore, since through God's mercy we have this ministry, we do not lose heart. Rather, we have renounced secret and shameful ways; we do not use deception, nor do we distort the word of God. On the contrary, by setting forth the truth plainly we commend ourselves to every man's conscience in the sight of God (2 Corinthians 3:18-4:2).

Verse 18 says we reflect our Lord's glory when we are transformed into his likeness. But what do we reflect if we aren't being transformed by God? We're still up front. We're still leaders. We're still playing in the band, singing in the choir, and even setting an example. But the leadership we display and the example we set are not godly if we are not being transformed by God.

Lord, since we are examples, make us the kind of examples that reflect you. Transform us to make us more like Jesus Christ. Help us to turn from secret sin and shameful practices. Keep our speech pure and true. Let others examine us as you examine us, and may they find us faithful. We are yours.

Example – Part 2

1 Corinthians 10 describes the freedom we have in Christ. But it's not as simple as a do-whatever-you-want approach. God gave his people, the Jews, specific guidelines about how to stay spiritually clean. But like we often do, they became distracted by the list of rules and forgot about its purpose: to help them understand the serious nature of sin and the joy of living the way God designed. Paul taught the Christians in Corinth about the balance between self-righteousness and haphazard immoral behavior.

"So whether you eat or drink or *whatever you do*, do it all for the glory of God. Do not cause anyone to stumble, whether Jews,

Greeks or the church of God - even as I try to please everybody in every way. For I am not seeking my own good but the good of many, so that they may be saved. Follow my example, as I follow the example of Christ" (1 Corinthians 10:31-11:1).

It's not about special dietary laws or ceremonial cleanliness. Rather than following a list of rules, God wants everything we do to glorify him. Then Paul took the issue one step further, noting the way our behavior affects others. Don't make others stumble, he said.

We are always setting an example. But we are not always setting a *good* one. Will moral choices benefit us? Of course, but they are not just for *our* own good. Our example of living a life that glorifies God benefits *others* too because it points their focus on God. Identify those who are following the example set by Jesus Christ, then follow suit.

Lord, make us the kind of examples that bring you glory and leads others to you. Don't let us get tied up in the rules. Free us to live the way you designed, free from sin, free from selfishness, free to love and enjoy life. Take whatever we do, and use it for your glory. Let us be an example to others about how we ought to live. We are yours.

Example – Part 3

What does it when I say a person's god is their stomach? Sometimes we get so caught up in our desires and appetites that we let them control us. We desire things, we desire experiences, we desire positions. I remember being so confused by the Scripture that says God will give us the desires of our hearts (Psalm 37:4) because I knew my heart desired some things that just weren't important to God. Then I learned the meaning of the first part of the verse. It isn't a free ticket to get whatever we want. It says, "Delight yourself in the Lord and he will give you the desires of your heart."

When the Lord is our delight, our heart desires him and everything he provides. But when our stomach, our appetite, or our insatiable desires for things of this world become our delight, we end up pursuing things that were never meant to satisfy.

Look at what Paul says is the destiny of those whose god is their stomach:

"Join with others in following my example, brothers, and take note of those who live according to the pattern we gave you. For, as I have often told you before and now say again even with tears, many live as *enemies* of the cross of Christ. *Their destiny is destruction*, their god is their stomach, and their glory is in their shame. Their mind is on earthly things. But our citizenship is in heaven. And we eagerly await a Savior from there, the Lord Jesus Christ, who, by the power that enables him to bring everything under his control, will transform our lowly bodies so that they will be like his glorious body" (Philippians 3:17-21).

Do you see the name given to those whose god is their stomach? They are called enemies of the cross of Christ. When we delight in the Lord, not only are we satisfied, but we are setting an example as partners with Christ. But the opposite is true as well. When we delight in our appetites, we can never be satisfied. And we make ourselves unhappy enemies of the cross.

Think about your desires. Think about your goals, hopes, and dreams as a worship leader. Do they align with delighting in our Lord or with your personal appetites?

Lord, like this Scripture says, help us to take note of those who live as examples of the pattern you gave us, delighting in you, and inviting you to transform us to become more and more like Jesus Christ. By this example, use us to point others toward you. We are yours.

Example – Part 4

I remember the first time I ever changed a baby's dirty diaper. Ew! If you've ever had the breath-taking pleasure of cleaning toxic explosions from an infant, you understand my reluctance to respond when my wife Adrian says, "Honey, will you check his diaper?" So how does a person transition from never changing a diaper to being a diaper-changing expert?

I've heard dads say they got away with never changing a diaper. But I didn't want to be that kind of dad (Common guys, suck it up!). But I also didn't want to admit how clueless I felt when it came to meeting my newborn son's basic needs. So just after his birth, there at the hospital, I waited until the next time a nurse changed him and I watched with eyes glues on everything she did. (I'll spare you the details here.)

Like everything else in life, I needed an example to follow. I need examples of other fathers. I need examples of other husbands. And I need examples of other Christians. Without the example that nurse set for me, I'd be a smelly mess! And without good examples of other Christ-followers, my spiritual journey would be a mess too!

Paul understood our need for examples. So he put himself on the spot and invited us to follow his example. He wasn't trying to impress us or get our attention focused on him. He said, follow me *as I follow Christ*. He knew we need examples to follow if we are to successfully live like Christ lived. But what exactly does Christ's example look like?

"If you suffer for doing good and you endure it, this is commendable before God. To this you were called, because Christ suffered for you, leaving you an example, that you should follow in his steps" 1 Peter 2:20-21.

It is far more convenient to think of the esteemed example to be one of moral character, biblical knowledge, faithful discipline, or sound theology and doctrine. While these things certainly are a part of the example Christ set for us, it was his willingness to *suffer for others* that makes following his example most difficult.

We are called to suffer. God asks us to think of others first. He expects us to be inconvenienced. If we are to truly follow (and set) the example of Christ, it must *cost* us something. What is it costing you now?

Is the example of Christ's suffering affecting your family? Does it impact your job? Does it influence your leisure time? Does it shape your decisions? Is it changing the way you think, dream, and live?

Lord, make us the kind of examples that reflect you. Make us more like Jesus Christ. Examine us and find us faithful. Help us see the kind of example we set, and shape us into the kind of example that brings you glory and leads others to you. Even when it costs us a great price, use our lives for your plan and purpose. We are yours.

Example – Part 5

One aspect of Paul's ministry was to help train and encourage new ministers like Timothy. He took Timothy under his wing, writing him letters about how to best follow Christ and bless others. Let's look together at one of the important lessons Paul taught him:

"Don't let anyone look down on you because you are young, but set an *example* for the believers in speech, in conduct, in love, in faith and in purity" (1 Timothy 4:12).

You may at times feel under-equipped or somehow inadequate to fulfill your ministry. So take Timothy's lesson to heart. No matter how long or short of a time you've been doing this, you can still set an example for others to follow.

How does Paul say Timothy will set a good example? Not by his age or the duration of his ministry. Paul taught Timothy to set an example for others in the things he said, the things he did, the way he displayed love, his faithfulness, and his purity from sinful living. This is our example to others.

In the same way, our lives should support our worship leading ministry in our speech, conduct, love, faith, and purity.

Lord, use us as good examples for others to follow, in the things we say, the way we conduct our lives, our love toward others, our faith, and our purity. Make us yours.

Example – Part 6

True or false: an example is the kind of behavior that others should follow.

"Now these things occurred as examples to keep us from setting our hearts on evil things as they did... These things happened to them as examples and were written down as warnings for us, on whom the culmination of the ages has come" (1 Corinthians 10:6, 11).

"Let us, therefore, make every effort to enter that rest, so that no one will perish by following their example of disobedience" (Hebrews 4:11).

"In a similar way, Sodom and Gomorrah and the surrounding towns gave themselves up to sexual immorality and perversion. They serve as an example of those who suffer the punishment of eternal fire" (Jude 1:7).

"Dear friend, do not imitate what is evil but what is good. Anyone who does what is good is from God. Anyone who does what is evil has not seen God" (3 John 1:11).

Each of these Scriptures talk about someone setting an example for someone else. But what else to these Scriptures have in common? They all talk about *bad* examples! The answer to the question above (whether examples are the kind of behavior others should follow) is *false*. Some examples should not be followed.

One way or another, we are an example to others. The question is what kind of example we will be. In many cases, the people of Israel set a poor example, as described here in 1 Corinthians and Hebrews. The people in the cities of Sodom and Gomorrah set bad examples of sinful living, as described here in Jude. And 3 John talks about selfish people in the church who were spreading malicious nonsense. These are obviously not the kind of examples we should follow.

Which kind of example to you want to be? Which kind are you?

Lord, shape our lives and ministry so that others can follow our example as we follow the example of Christ and other godly people. Remove all sin from us. Take away selfishness. Don't let bad attitude or hurtful speech have any place in what we do. Make us your example. Make us yours.

Example – Part 7

When we step into a leadership role – like leading worship – people quickly begin to look at us in a new way. Fair or not, we are held to a higher standard as leaders. Everything we do and say (and the way we do and say those things) is placed under microscopic scrutiny.

Have you ever been critical of someone who is in leadership? What if those same standards of excellence or perfection were applied to you?

Let's look at how Scripture says we should carefully lead.

"Whatever you do or say, do it as a representative of the Lord Jesus, giving thanks through him to God the Father" (Colossians 3:17).

As followers, our choices effect our reputation. As leaders, our choices effect God's reputation. The difference is that we become *representatives* of Jesus Christ. When people see us, they are supposed to see Jesus within us. Let's keep this in mind when we are in front of other people (and when we aren't).

Lord, help us to set a good example so that our words and actions will lead people toward you. Use us as a good example that other people can follow and grow closer to you. We are yours.

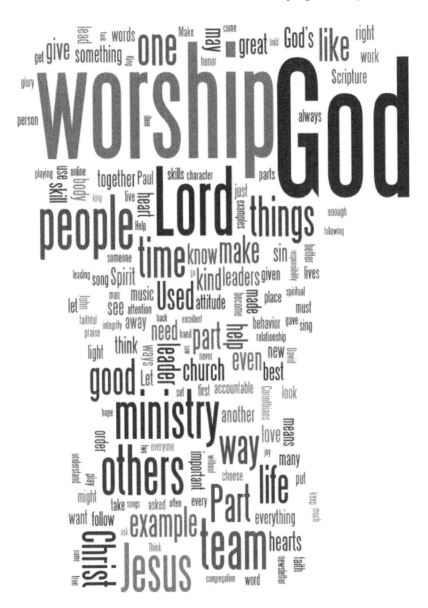

Skill – Part 1

Take a moment to be perfectly quiet. What do you hear? There is constantly ambient noise all around us. But our minds ignore these sounds. Why, because they're unimportant? No, we tend to ignore most ambient noise because it's constantly there.

BANG! Did you hear that? The introduction of a new sound is quickly noticed above the ambient noise because it is dynamically different.

Skilled musicians use dynamics. They understand the value of a quiet rest, the value of a soft note, and the value of loud noise. The difference between these sounds is called dynamics.

Novice musicians often make the mistake of playing or singing every note, every chord, every word. When they are asked to rest during a stanza, they sometimes become offended, not understanding the value of the rest.

Shaping Worship

When all we do is play all the time, we become the ambient noise that others ignore. Lack of dynamics makes us poor worship leaders.

Believe it or not, Scripture talks about the important skill of dynamics in music. Look at it with me in 1 Corinthians 14:7:

"Even in the case of lifeless things that make sounds, such as the flute or harp, how will anyone know what tune is being played unless there is a distinction in the notes?"

Blah, blah, blah! Don't let your voice or instrument blur into oblivion. Pay attention to when your sheet music or leader asks you to rest, play or sing quietly, and play or sing loudly. Implementing dynamics will make you a better worship leader.

Lord, help us to understand the importance of resting, playing quietly, and playing loudly. When we should rest, we will rest. When we should be quiet, we will be quiet. When we should be loud, we will be loud. Help us to use dynamics as a skill of leading worship. Make us yours.

Skill – Part 2

Rewriting music is a skill practiced by many worship leaders, including the psalmists, David and Asaph. Throughout their psalms, you'll find instructions for how they intended their works to be sung "to the tune of" other songs (9, 22, 45, 56-60, 69, 75, and 80).

Some of your favorite songs may be rewritten and you might not even realize it. A quick glance in the back of many hymnals will take you to a tool called the metrical index. A song can be sung to the tune of any other song with a matching meter (rhythm and syllables). You'll also find the index of tune names in the back of many hymnals, showing multiple songs that actually share the same melody, harmony, rhythm, and key.

Sometimes a song is rewritten by giving new lyrics to an existing tune. Other times the lyrics stay the same, but the tune and / or rhythm are changed. This can be done with Scripture (setting the words to new music), worship songs (setting the words to a new tune), and even secular radio songs (massaging the lyrics to make them suitable for the church).

There was a time when Paul visited the city Athens. He was troubled when he saw people giving their worship to false gods and idols. When a group of Greek philosophers asked Paul to explain his sermons, he spoke to them in ways they would understand, by referring to the Greek god Zeus and quoting their secular works (*Epimenides* and *Aratus*). He took what was secular, and sanctified it for a divine purpose (See Acts 17 and Titus 1:12).

Lord, open our ears and creative imaginations to help us see opportunities to use music in new ways. Use the songs we hear and sing for your divine purpose. Make them fresh and new. By your Holy Spirit, let these songs speak your truth in our hearts and lives. We are yours.

Skill – Part 3

"Sing to him a new song; play skillfully, and shout for joy" (Psalm 33:3).

There is a delicate balance between too much and too little new music. New songs have pros and cons. Can you think of some?

The pros include fresh ways of expressing our hearts of worship, fulfilling the Scripture to "sing a new song." They lift us from the mundane, the mindless, and the mediocre. But new songs have cons too, including the difficulty of engaging in worship. When a person doesn't know the lyrics, rhythm, or melody of a new song, they often disengage from worship and simply become *observers*.

As worship leaders (not observer leaders) our responsibility is to help people engage in worship.

One important skill for the worship leader to learn is how to introduce new songs with skill and joy. This is one of the many skills required (and commanded) for leading worship.

Every band I've ever played with has always had trouble the first run through a new song. Some are better than others. But we're sure to butcher at least part (if not all) of it the first try. If at first you don't succeed, then don't introduce a new song to your congregation until you (and your band) have had plenty of time to *practice* and *master* the new song.

One way to test whether you've practiced enough and are finally ready to pull out that new song is to ask yourself: Do we enjoy playing this song? One aspect of music that many musicians appreciate involves the rules that govern the sound. There are some notes that sound good together (we call them chords).

There is an established rhythm, tempo, timing, and progression for each song. But wait – I'm describing the technical details of mastering the song, just after asking whether we *enjoy* playing it? Yes. The reason is simple: music is more pleasing when it is played well, with skill. If you don't enjoy playing a new song, you probably haven't mastered it yet.

So take the time, put forth the effort, and learn that new song. Then when you're ready, sing it for our Lord. Teach it to his congregation. Play it with skill. And enjoy it.

Lord, help us to learn and master new music so that we can play it skillfully and with joy. Help us to find the right balance between reusing old music and introducing new songs. Make us masters of this music so we can enjoy it and help others to enjoy it with us. We are yours.

Skill – Part 4

After David, there was a king named Josiah. Scripture tells us that he did what God thought was right. He sought God and tried to help everyone in his kingdom to turn away from sin. One of the many ways he did this was to ask a group of others to restore the Temple. Using money collected from the people, these leaders hired workers - carpenters, stone masons, musicians, paper pushers, and more.

"The men did the work *faithfully*. Over them to direct them were Jahath and Obadiah, Levites... The Levites - all who were *skilled* in playing musical instruments - had charge of the laborers and supervised all the workers from job to job. Some of the Levites were secretaries, scribes and doorkeepers" (2 Chronicles 34:12-13).

There are two descriptions here that we should notice, faithful and skilled. These workers were entrusted with an important task: restoring the place of worship, maximizing it to its potential so others could come and worship our Lord there. They were faithful to do this work. And they brought their skill to the job.

Our faithfulness in our ministry happens in the moment. Our skill happens in what we do that leads up to those moments. Both are important aspects of worship ministry. When we arrive on time and fulfill our role in ministry, we are being faithful. When we practice and prepare, we are building skill.

When we are at home, alone, apart from the church and our worship team, spending time singing, playing an instrument, practicing scales or solos, this kind of preparation is a form worship because it builds our skill as worship leaders. When we are in worship, with others, among the church and our worship team, singing, playing an instrument, and using what we have practiced, this is a form of worship because it demonstrates our faithfulness to serve.

Lord, make us faithful and skilled worship leaders. Help us find opportunities to prepare and advance ours skill as worshippers. Find us faithful as we bring our skill to the ministry. Make us yours.

Skill – Part 5

Have you ever heard the phrase "It's good enough for who it's for"? It means even though something isn't perfect, if it's being done for someone who doesn't care, then the imperfection doesn't matter. It's an excuse to be sloppy, lazy, or half-hearted.

This is not the kind of worship God expects. When we consider who our worship is for, suddenly "good enough" just doesn't quite seem good enough. Our worship should be the best!

"Clap your hands, all you nations; shout to God with cries of joy. How awesome is the Lord Most High, the great King over all the earth! God has ascended amid shouts of joy, the Lord amid the sounding of trumpets. Sing praises to God, sing praises; sing praises to our King, sing praises. For God is the King of all the earth; sing to him a psalm* of praise" (Psalm 47:1-2, 5-7).

* The word translated "psalm" here is *maskil*. It means to sing with understanding and skill. The NASB translates this line as "Sing praises with a skillful psalm."

When we plan, prepare for, and perform worship, we should always consider who it's for. We should obey this scriptural admonition to sing a maskil – a song with understanding and skill. Be careful to understand the lyrics you sing. Sing and play skillfully so that our worship will be acceptable to the Most High God.

Lord, we will offer to you a maskil, a song of understanding and skill. We will practice, prepare, and perfect new skills for you. Let our musical accomplishments reflect how wonderful we think you are. Make us the best worship leaders, the best worshippers, for you are the best, Lord God. Make us yours.

Skill – Part 6

David was a good king because he was a good shepherd. It sounds odd, especially considering the different skill-sets required for either job. But I don't believe it was the skills of shepherding that necessarily enabled David to develop the skills of being king. Instead, I think it had more to do with his attitude. Listen to the description of David's attitude in this psalm:

"David shepherded them with *integrity* of heart; with skillful hands he led them" (Psalms 78:72).

Did you catch the word in that line that communicates attitude? It's integrity. David worked to develop the necessary skills for the jobs God asked him to do. He didn't fake his way through it. He didn't try to hide his weakness. He maintained integrity. Whether that meant using the skill of finding safe pasture or the skill of settling domestic disputes, David coupled integrity with his skill.

In our ministry, we should have the same attitude. We practice and prepare to develop our skill. We face our weakness and failure with integrity, learning from our mistakes and improving our skill. Be a shepherd with integrity. Lead with skillful hands.

Lord, give us integrity in our hearts and skill in our hands so that we might serve you and your people through this ministry. Help us to learn and improve our skills. When people see and hear our ministry, direct their hearts to praise and thank you. We are yours.

Skill – Part 7

In the book of Exodus, we read the story about how God freed his people from Egyptian slavery. Once they were no longer slaves to Egypt, they established a covenant relationship with God. He would be their God, leading and protecting them; and they would be his people, following and obeying him. The rules God gave his people helped them to live within the boundaries of that covenant relationship.

Some of those rules pertained specifically to worship. Our experience in worship constantly shapes our lives so that we live in covenant relationship with our God. Let's read a line taken from the instructions about worship and covenant relationship.

"Instruct all the *skilled* craftsmen whom I have *filled* with the spirit of wisdom. Have them make garments for Aaron that will distinguish him as a priest set apart for my service" (Exodus 28:3 NLT).

What word is used to describe the craftsmen who would design the priestly clothes used in worship? Skilled. God chose skilled people for this important task in worship.

Anyone can learn a new skill (some of us may do it faster or better than others). So what set these skilled worked apart from the rest? Why were they chosen to design worship clothes for the priest? In addition to being skilled, they were also filled with the spirit of wisdom. We need to be skilled and filled. The first word in this text is "instruct." Even the craftsmen who were greatly skilled still needed to be filled with additional instruction and wisdom to fulfill their role.

Lord, instruct us in the areas of our skill. Fill us with wisdom. Use our skilled-and-filled hearts in worship to enable others – priests, pastors, and worshippers - to worship in ways that honor you, build up your people, and shape us to live in covenant relationship with you. Make us yours.

Excellence – Part 1

Several years back I made a New Year's resolution to work out. Early in January, my friend John and I went to the gym together where I discovered a device called the Roman Chair. It's a piece of exercise equipment designed to work your leg and stomach muscles. I saw others doing 10 or 20 repetitions and then quit. "Pbbbbt! That looks easy!" I said to myself. Then I proceeded to make one of the stupidest exercise mistakes possible. Since I enjoyed the Roman Chair and since I wanted to impress my friend John with my supreme muscular tone, I put in about 80 repetitions in a row. Later that afternoon, my stomach muscles felt a little sore. Little did I know that I would wake up in pain every day for the next three weeks!

The New Year prompts many of us to resolve to be better people, establish better habits, eat better vegetables, and say better words. This holiday is a good reminder to us of things we should be trying to do throughout the whole year.

But if you're anything like me, your resolutions have a slippery way of falling apart. I never went back to the gym that year. I suppose I could have, after my stomach quit hurting so much. But I weaseled my way out of my commitment saying, "I agreed to workout; I didn't say how many times."

Genesis 4 tells the story of two brothers, one who did his best and one who did not. Let's look at it together.

"Now Abel kept flocks, and Cain worked the soil. In the course of time Cain brought some of the fruits of the soil as an offering to the Lord. But Abel brought fat portions from some of the firstborn of his flock. The Lord looked with favor on Abel and his offering, but on Cain and his offering he did not look with favor. So Cain was very angry, and his face was downcast. Then the Lord said to Cain, 'Why are you angry? Why is your face downcast? If you *do what is right*, will you not be accepted? But if you do not do what is right, sin is crouching at your door; it desires to have you, but you must master it'" (2-7).

When it comes to making resolutions (at the New Year and all year long), take God's advice to Cain: do what is right. He deserves our best, not our leftovers. Will you put him first?

Lord, help us to stop making excuses for ourselves. When you convict us to implement changes in our lives, help us resolve to follow through. Help us to learn from the story of Cain and Abel, and to do what is right. Make us yours.

Excellence – Part 2

God deserves our best. So we choose to bring our best efforts to him and to his church. What does our best look like? The answer will be unique to each of us, but still has some commonalities worth noting. Look at the table below and identify which side is best.

Showing up for worship tired from last night's movie marathon	Showing up for worship after getting proper rest
Only picking up your instrument when you practice with the band once a week	Rehearsing songs until you are ready, even if it means spending your own time to prepare
Wearing your favorite shirt to worship, knowing it has an offensive image / words on it	Wearing clothes that honor God and the congregation

Saying whatever comes to mind	Filtering your speech, speaking with love, avoiding crude language
Complaining	Sharing your frustrations in a respectful way in an attempt to improve things

When we choose to bring our best to God, it shows what we think of him. The opposite is also true. When we choose to bring our not-so-best to God, this shows what we think of him too. Read what Jesus thinks of you, from Matthew 5:14-16.

"You are the light of the world. A city on a hill cannot be hidden. Neither do people light a lamp and put it under a bowl. Instead they put it on its stand, and it gives light to everyone in the house. In the same way, let your light shine before men, that they may see your good deeds and praise your Father in heaven."

The purpose of the light is not to draw attention to itself. It does not shine so people will notice how bright and lovely it is. The light shines so that others can see what the light shines *upon.*

As lead worshippers, we're like a light that is placed on a stand. We either shine light upon our God or upon ourselves. When we choose not to give God our best, it's like covering up that light. It's like shining the light on ourselves instead of shining on God.

When we're tired, lazy, or unprepared for worship, people are not pointed towards God by our dim lights. They are dangerously pointed toward us. When we don't give our best in practice and preparation, our mistakes don't shine on God. Instead they draw people's attention to our dim lights. In the same way, when our speech, appearance, behavior, or attitudes don't point people to God, we are not being worship leaders; we're being self-worshippers.

So let your light – your best light – shine before other people so that they may see your good actions, words, and attitudes, and as a result, praise our Father in heaven.

Lord, make us a light that shines brightly on you. We commit to give you our best. This includes our time, energy, decisions, attitudes, behavior, and speech. Use our lives and our ministry to shine brightly upon you so others can see you and worship you. Make us yours.

Excellence – Part 3

We've talked before about how you are a leader. Yes, you.

You have influence over your family, your neighbors, your friends, your relatives, your coworkers, your schoolmates, etc. Whether you do it intentionally or not, you influence others. And as a follower of Christ, your influence should be Christ-like.

So what exactly does that look like for you and me in real life?

In his first letter to Timothy, Paul gave descriptions of good leaders in the church. The character-requirements Paul listed include issues related to behavior, family and relationships, attitudes, habits, experience, reputation, and integrity.

Let's identify how each issue affects a person's character. Think about how the word on the left-side of the table below can be an indicator of a person's character. Reflect on each character requirement on the left, then read the right side of the table.

Character Requirements	How the requirement affects character
Behavior	Character affects choices, which, in turn affect our behavior. When we have poor behavior, it is evidence of poor character.
Family / Relationships	The character of our closest friends and family often reflects upon our character, showing the kind of influence we have on others around us.
Attitudes	God gave us a large variety of emotions. How we choose to respond to those emotions is called *attitude*. When negative emotions grow into negative attitudes, it reflects negative character.
Habits	Habits are behaviors that we choose to repeat, whether consciously or not. In the same way poor behavior reflects poor character, so do poor habits.

Character Requirements	How the requirement affects character
Experience	Behavior and attitudes can be temporarily faked. But experience over time shows evidence of a person's true character.
Reputation	As our behavior and attitudes affect others, we earn a reputation, for good or bad. Our reputation may not always be completely accurate, but is an indicator of our character.
Integrity	When we say one thing but do something else, or act differently based on our audience, we lack integrity. A person of good character strives for integrity.

These seven character requirements from 1 Timothy 3 are good tests of our character. I encourage you to read the whole chapter and think about what each one indicates in your character.

1 Timothy 3:13 says, "Those who have served well gain an excellent standing and great assurance in their faith in Christ Jesus."

Lord, help us to serve well. Let our behavior honor you. Let our relationships reflect our relationship with you. Let our attitudes be the same as Jesus Christ. Let our habits grow from the direction of your Spirit in our hearts. Use these character-revealing aspects of our lives to build the experience, reputation, and integrity of excellent leaders. Make us yours.

Excellence – Part 4

Think about the word devotion. If I devote my time every Wednesday evening to prepare for Sunday worship, I am *giving* that time up, *dedicating* it for a specific purpose, *relinquishing* my rights to that time. Give, dedicate, and relinquish are words that help us understand the word devotion.

"This is a trustworthy saying. And I want you to stress these things, so that those who have trusted in God may be careful to *devote* themselves to doing what is *good.* These things are *excellent* and *profitable* for everyone." (Titus 3.8)

There are three words used to describe what we are called to be devoted to: good, excellent, and profitable. Let's do as this Scripture says: devote ourselves to doing things that are good, excellent, and profitable. How do we do this? Give, dedicate, and relinquish.

What are you already giving for this ministry? What more could you give of yourself to do what is good, excellent, and profitable?

What are the signs of your dedication to this ministry? What is keeping you from taking the next step of full dedication?

What have you had to relinquish (stop or give up) in order to do what is good, excellent, and profitable for this ministry?

Lord, you deserve the most excellent praise. We choose to give our best for you, not the left-overs, not the extra, not the convenient. Make us fully dedicated to you. Show us what we need to relinquish in order to do things that are good, excellent, and profitable for this ministry. We are yours.

Excellence – Part 5

Have you ever thought to yourself any of the following statements?

- No one will be able to tell if I take this short cut in ministry.
- It's okay if I mess this little part up, because it isn't very important to my ministry.
- There are more important things I could be doing in ministry.

Each statement has something in common. They neglect the importance of excellence in ministry. Excellence says we never take short cuts, whether people notice or not. Excellence means there are no little parts or big parts of ministry; it's all important. Excellence is treating everything in ministry as the important thing.

Jesus told a story in Matthew 25 about a man who entrusted money to three people. Each person was given a specific amount – big, medium, or small. He expected them to invest the funds while he was away traveling. Then when he returned, he asked for an account of their investments.

The first two people did exactly as the man had hoped. They earned interest on the investments. He responded to them,

"Well done, good and faithful servant! You have been faithful with a few things; I will put you in charge of many things. Come and share your master's happiness!" (Matthew 25:21).

But the third person had not been faithful with the small amount they were given. Perhaps they thought it didn't matter because the amount was so small. Or maybe they thought there was something better they could have been doing with their time and energy.

The rest of this story in Matthew 25:14-30 tells us that the small amount of money was taken away from him and given to the one who had earned the most interest. Then he was kicked out, forced to leave the group entirely.

Lord, help us to see what we do as an important part of ministry. Do not let us look down on ourselves, even for the small and simple things that we do. Use what we offer, and make it increase for your glory. Maximize our investment for you. Multiply our efforts for you. Make our lives and our ministry an excellent act of worship for you. We are yours.

Excellence – Part 6

Our Lord has high standards for everything we do. Unfortunately, we often underestimate God's standards when we do things for him. Psalm 96 speaks to this topic:

"Sing to the Lord a new song; sing to the Lord, all the earth. Sing to the Lord, praise his name; proclaim his salvation day after day. Declare his glory among the nations, his marvelous deeds among all peoples. For great is the Lord and most worthy of praise; he is to be feared above all gods" (v 1-4).

Some translations say, "the Lord is great, and greatly to be praised" (and is to be praised greatly). Others say, "we owe him great praise." Any way you look at it, he is a great God; and he deserves the best kind of worship we could possibly offer.

If I were to put these lyrics into my own words, they would say:

"Sing something new to the Lord. Everyone should sing. Sing about his great reputation. Sing about his great salvation. Never stop singing. Use your music as a way to tell others how

135

glorious our Lord is. Our Lord is great. So give him great praise!"

Lord, we commit to offering you excellent worship. We will join with your people in singing your praise. You are a great God who does great things. We celebrate your salvation and your glorious works. You are worthy of my greatest praise. We are yours.

Excellence – Part 7

"Therefore, since we are receiving a kingdom that cannot be shaken, let us be thankful, and so *worship God acceptably* with reverence and awe, for our God is a consuming fire" (Hebrews 12:28-29).

What does it mean to worship God acceptably? To answer this question we must understand what kind of worship God accepts. How would you describe the kind of worship that you think is acceptable to God?

We know that the kind of religion God accepts involves caring for others who are in need (James 1:27). And we know that God seeks worshippers who will worship him in spirit and truth

(John 4:23). From this text in Hebrews we see that acceptable worship involves two things: reverence and awe.

Neither of these are words we use in our everyday vocabulary. Reverence involves deep respect, honor, and adoration. Awe is more commonly used as a prefix in the word awesome. To show awe is to show that you think something is awesome, impressive, or amazing.

Determining whether our worship meets these criteria requires a bit of self-examination. Ask yourself:

- Is my worship characterized by deep respect for God (and other worshippers)?
- Who receives the most honor from my worship?
- What do I adore most about worship? (If my answer isn't God, then am I worshipping him or something else?).
- Is my worship characterized by a sense of awe? Do I truly believe that God is awesome and impressive? Or have I lost my wonder and amazement in him?

Would an outside observer give the same answers when describing you from the questions above? Would God?

Shaping Worship

Lord, let your holy fire burn away anything in us that isn't acceptable to you. We want our worship and our lives to honor you. Restore our sense of adoration and awe. You are amazing God. Make us yours.

Team – Part 1

How might you rate yourself on the following scales? Pick the number that matches the closest to your actions in regard to the worship ministry. (You have permission to make copies of this page for your team).

Devoted to self	4	3	2	1	Devoted to one another
Doesn't worry about being on time	4	3	2	1	Tries to be on time
Gives a "good enough" effort	4	3	2	1	Gives the best effort
Doesn't own up to mistakes / failures	4	3	2	1	Learns from mistakes / failures
Earns a reputation of being unreliable	4	3	2	1	Earns a reputation of being dependable
Inflexible, not a team player	4	3	2	1	Flexible, thinking of the team over self

What keeps you from scoring more on the right? Identifying what holds you back could reveal what needs to change in order to help make you a better worship leader.

In Romans 12, Paul describes a life of worship as pleasing to God. The evidence of such a life is found in the following verses:

"Be devoted to one another in brotherly love. Honor one another above yourselves. Never be lacking in zeal, but keep your spiritual fervor, serving the Lord. Be joyful in hope, patient in affliction, faithful in prayer" (Romans 12:10-12).

The text begins with the instruction to be devoted to one another. Think of how the actions on the right side of the list all related to devotion to this team. The second instruction in the text is to honor one another above yourselves. How can we do this, practically speaking? This may mean honoring others in the ministry, or honoring others in the congregation over the team. The third instruction is about zeal and fervor – passionate enthusiasm. These are both very much a part of the ministry of worship.

Let's use this text as our prayer.

Lord, make us devoted to this team in brotherly love. Help us to honor one another above ourselves. Fill us with zeal and fervor, passionate enthusiasm about worshipping and serving you. Fill us with joy and hope, patience and endurance, and faithfulness. Make us yours.

Team – Part 2

Any time one human being is in contact with another human being, there is bound to be conflict. Our God made us each unique. We think, act, speak, and feel differently. This is a good and beautiful thing. But our differences often lead to disagreement. How we handle that disagreement reveals what kind of people we really are.

The worship band or choir can either be a *collection of individuals*, or it can be a *team*. What is the difference between the two? A collection of individuals meets at the same time, in the same place, doing the same (or similar) things. Yet they remain a collection of individuals. This is a recipe for conflict.

On the other hand, if the worship band or choir chooses to become a team, they meet at the same time (respecting the time of others in the group), in the same place (respecting the space given to us for what we do), doing the same thing (in agreement with each other, for a common purpose and goal). This kind of team has an identity as a whole, not as a collection of individuals.

Have you ever done or said something that hurt another person in the worship band or choir? Have your prioritized your schedule over theirs, choosing to be late or absent? Have you prioritized your personal preferences over theirs, demanding your way, your style, or your songs? These are the symptoms that we are acting as a collection of individuals instead of acting as a team.

So what should we do? James 5 says,

"Confess your sins to each other and pray for each other…"

It sounds nice. But it gets even better. The next line tells us why we should confess and pray with one another:

"…so that you may be healed. The prayer of a righteous [person] is powerful and effective" (16).

It's not always easy for us to get along. So let's work together as a team, remembering we aren't perfect. Let's be honest with ourselves and the rest of the team. And if there's a conflict, let's discuss it up front instead of letting it grow.

Lord, make us team-players. Help us to put others first, so the team can benefit, even when we do not. Prod us with your Spirit to maintain unity with this team through confession and prayer. We are yours.

Team – Part 3

2 Chronicles 35 describes all of the work King Josiah organized in order to celebrate the Passover, one of the most important festivals of Jewish worship. He gave instructions to the priests about how God expected them to lead worship, and "encouraged them in their work at the Temple of the Lord" (2).

Over thirty-thousand sheep, lambs, goats, and bulls were sacrificed (7-9). In a prescribed ritual, they were skinned and their blood was sprinkled on the altar. Some would be completely consumed as Whole Burnt Offerings, a symbol of complete submission to the Lord. Others were roasted and boiled to be eaten as a symbol of God's saving acts for his people (10-13).

Josiah passed on the instructions left by King David: "Take your place in the sanctuary - a team of Levites for every grouping of your fellow citizens, the laity. Your job is to kill the Passover lambs, then consecrate yourselves and prepare the lambs so that everyone will be able to keep the Passover exactly as God commanded through Moses" (5-6 MSG).

With so much happening at such a huge worship celebration, everyone had their place; everyone had a responsibility to fulfill. Some dealt with the sacrifices, others led singing and music, and some kept guard at each gate (15). It took them all morning, all afternoon, and late into the evening to prepare for this seven-day worship festival (14).

King Josiah got the priests, the Levites, the musicians, the singers, the guards, and all the people of Jerusalem, Judah, and Israel to work together *as a team* to orchestrate one of the greatest celebrations of worship since the time of the prophet Samuel!

When we gather for congregational worship, there are many things that happen, many roles to fill. There are some who greet worshippers at the doors. Some pass out bulletins, typed information about worship. There are some who collect an offering from God's people to be given to his church. Announcements are shared. Prayers are requested. Skilled instruments are played. And sermons are preached.

Outside of those who are busy serving on Sunday mornings is a whole host of people who work to prepare for congregational worship. Our pastor seeks the Lord in order to deliver a message from God to his people. Scripture readings are selected. Songs are written, arranged, and practiced. Videos are created, edited, and cued. Lyrics are typed. Group prayers are composed. Floors are cleaned. Phone calls are made. Coffee beans are ground. And tables are wiped off. More and more and more than we can imagine goes into preparing for just one week of congregational worship. What a wonderful way to honor our Lord.

Thank you! To everyone who gives time, energy, and skill to organize worship, thank you. You are a part of the body of Christ. To every group that sacrifices for the sake of the congregation, thank you. You are a part of a team fulfilling God's design for our lives. Let us continue spurring each other on as we worship our Lord together!

Lord, unite our team of worship leaders together in our common purpose. Just as Josiah organized many people to prepare for and lead worship long ago, help us to work together, bringing together all the details. Let our teamwork honor you and bless your people. We are yours.

Team – Part 4

Once I had a rock polishing kit. You'd put crummy looking rocks in it, add some sand, and a few irritating days later you've got beautiful, smooth stones. The sand and rocks rub against each other until their rough edges are worn off. But it takes days for this process to complete. And if rocks had feelings, I'm sure they'd be saying "OUCH!" the whole time.

People are like those rocks, covered by rough edges. Each of us has weaknesses, mistakes, and failures. Sometimes our rough edges grate against those around us, poking others with our imperfections, opinions, and judgments. This can be painful!

Now take a group of imperfect people and put them together with a common goal. We can't yet call them a "team" as long as they continue to act like a group of individuals. So what is it that makes a team a team? How can the rough rocks become smooth stones?

A team works together to share responsibility, putting others before self. The individuals on a team use their strengths to benefit the team. And when the rough edges begin to poke others on the team, they endure the painful process knowing it will produce a better team.

Being part of a team doesn't mean always agreeing. In fact, when we work as a team, our differences take on a tremendous potential. Instead of hurting those around us, our imperfections can rub away the rough edges, leaving better people than before.

"As iron sharpens iron, so one man sharpens another" (Proverbs 27:17).

Will you commit to work together as a team? Will you offer grace to your team members when their rough edges poke you? Will you do your best to let your strengths benefit the team? Will you endure the team-shaping process?

Lord, use us as a part of your church, your team. Take our strengths and skills and use them for your team. Take our weaknesses, and help us through the refining process. Give us the grace we need to be team players. We are yours.

Team – Part 5

David wrote about the deep pain he experienced as enemies attacked. We can quickly empathize with his emotional response. All of us have been hurt at one time or another.

Here are two columns. The left column is copied directly from Psalm 41 (NIV). The right column is a paraphrase in conversational vocabulary.

6 Whenever one [an enemy] comes to see me, he speaks falsely,	6 Sometimes because of ignorance, other times because of sinful motives, they say things that are not true.
while his heart gathers slander; then he goes out and spreads it abroad.	They are always watching for me to do something wrong. And when they think they've found it, they go and tell others to make more enemies for me.
7 All my enemies whisper together against me;	7 Rather than speaking with me about the conflict, they talk behind my back with their friends.
they imagine the worst for me, saying,	They want me to fail.
8 "A vile disease has beset him; he will never get up from the place where he lies."	8 They think I'm a failure. I can never improve in their eyes.

It doesn't surprise us much to hear about enemies treating David this way. We expect nothing less from an enemy. But David wasn't just talking about his enemies. Read the next verse:

"Even my close friend, whom I trusted, he who shared my bread, has lifted up his heel against me" (Psalm 41:9).

Friends have far more potential to hurt us than enemies because they are close to us – close enough to see our weakness, see our faults, see which buttons to push. We expect our enemies to hurt us. And we expect our friends not to. So when friends let us down, it can hurt worse than when an enemy does.

This is part of the reason commitment to team ministry is so important. Your friends on this ministry team are counting on you. The team will not always agree on everything. There will be conflict, misunderstanding, miscommunication, and even hurt feelings. Yet as a member of this important team, you cannot afford to act like an enemy.

Lord, build this team, starting with me. Train our eyes to watch for the success of our teammates, not their failure. Stop us from spreading slander about our team. Don't let us talk behind another team member's back. Help us always make room for the team to improve. Make us yours.

Team – Part 6

Playing in a worship band, leading worship for a church is a privilege, not a right. It's a gift when God uses something we enjoy doing (playing music and singing) to serve and minister to others. Let's read about how Scripture says we should treat this kind of gift.

"So it is with you. Since you are eager to have spiritual gifts, try to excel in gifts that build up the church" (1 Corinthians 14:12).

Desiring to play in a worship band or sing in a choir is a good thing. It's a desire to participate in a spiritual act: worship. It's a desire to have a privileged opportunity (a gift) to lead. "Since you are eager to have a spiritual gift," this Scripture says, "try to excel in gifts that" do what? *Build up the church.*

When we talk about being a part of a worship team, we don't just mean the musicians and singers. Your congregation is as much a part of a team as the guitar player. Who would you be leading if the congregation were absent?

This being the case, we need to keep the team - the whole team - in mind as we lead worship. When my-way-or-the-highway attitudes are born, we stop being leaders because we stop considering the team.

Lord, help us to build up your church as we lead worship. Remind us that this ministry is a gift that you've given us. And help the things we do, say, sing, and play work together to bless your church. We are yours.

Team – Part 7

Take a moment to consider the things you do that contribute to the worship ministry. Perhaps you sing, play an instrument, copy sheet music, type lyrics, setup speakers, or organize video projection, etc. Each person on the team has a part to play. What is yours?

Now that you've reflected on your part, consider the role of the team leader. He or she probably does many of the same things you do, and then *a whole lot more*. Think about how things go when they are absent (ill, vacation, etc.). What gets left undone? What gets done poorly when they are gone? They carry a lot more weight than you may realize.

Jesus and his disciples acted as a ministry team, just like we do. Each disciple contributed their part. But it wasn't always that way. When they first joined the team, they spent most of their time *watching* Jesus do the work, *listening* to him make decisions and give direction, *following* him wherever he went. Then one day, that all changed.

Jesus had just received the sad news of John the Baptist's death. Understandably, he withdrew to spend some time alone. But his celebrity status wouldn't allow for private time. A crowd of people followed him, unsympathetic to his emotional state. Instead of being angry or frustrated, Jesus had compassion on them and healed their illnesses.

When evening came, the disciples suggested that Jesus should send the people back to the village so they could feed themselves. But he said no. "They do not need to go away. You give them something to eat" (Matthew 14:16).

Jesus knew it was unhealthy for the disciples to sit back and watch as he did all the work. He chose to involve them, making them ministry partners with him. The end result was a miracle that fed over 5,000. In the same way, we cannot rely on the worship pastor or choir director to do all the dirty work for us. We all have a responsibility as a part of this team. Can you hear Christ saying it to you? "You give them something to eat."

Lord, use us as a part of this ministry team. When we see something that needs done, prompt us to take initiative. Make us your ministry partner, our team leader's partner, and our team's partner. Make us yours.

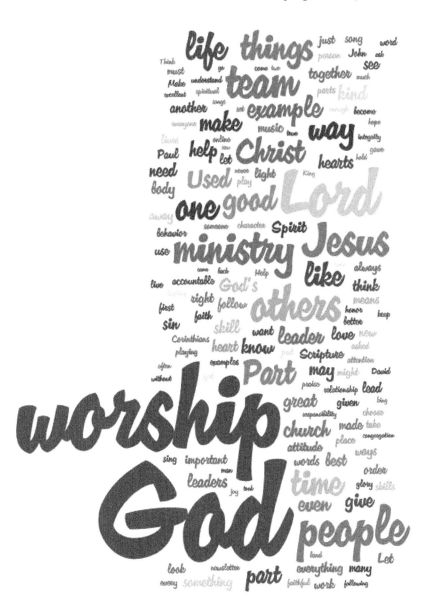

Submission - Part 1

Personally, I think feet are gross. Even if they're clean with
neatly trimmed nails, they still seem gross to me. Now crank
that up a notch... a few days ago I saw a picture display from a
local podiatrist. Malformed, infected, broken, sprained, injured,
and more – the images turned my stomach. GROSS!

Yet if you've ever walked across a dark room and stubbed your
pinky toe on some furniture, you understand how one tiny body
part can quickly and powerfully affect the rest of the whole
body. Every body part, even the small gross ones, needs to be
healthy and performing their function in order for the rest of
the body to function in a healthy way.

Scripture uses this same body-parts-analogy to describe the
church: "God arranged the parts in the body, every one of
them, just as he wanted them to be" (1 Corinthians 12:18). The
text goes on to point out how foolish it would be for one body
part to claim they don't need the other parts. Can the eye listen?
Can the ear taste? Can the mouth hear? Of course not.

As a Christian, you are a part of Christ's body. *But you don't get to choose which part. God does.* By including you in his body, the church, God asks you to be responsible and accountable to the other body parts. You can't survive without them. And they can't fully function without you.

Lord, we choose to submit to your body, knowing this is part of the way we submit to you. Help us accept the role you've designed for us to play - even if that means we are a gross foot. We are yours.

Submission – Part 2

We've already read the biblical description of the church working like body parts arranged by God (1 Corinthians 12:18). And we understand that in order for the whole body to function in a healthy way, some parts lead and other parts follow. This doesn't make one part any better than another. It simply follows the organization that God establishes. Let's read more about what this means.

"Obey your leaders and submit to their authority. They keep watch over you as men who must give an account. Obey them so that their work will be a joy, not a burden, for that would be of no advantage to you" (Hebrews 13:17).

Whose responsibility is it to keep a one-year-old child from playing in the road? The child's parents. The mother and father are responsible to nourish, instruct, and protect the child. In the same way, God has established leaders over us: government, police, bosses, parents, etc.

How would it feel to you as a boss in the workplace when your employee refuses to obey your instruction regarding completion of legal paperwork? Even if you don't work as a boss in an office, you can imagine the feelings of frustration, fear, and the great burden described in this text from Hebrews.

Our Lord asks us to obey our leaders and submit to their authority. This means doing what they ask, without complaining, even when we may disagree with them (unless they are asking us to do something unethical, immoral, or illegal). When you choose to follow the leaders God has established over you, then you are choosing to follow God.

Lord, help us to make our leader(s) feel joy as we obey and submit to them. Let our speech, behavior, and attitude reflect well upon our leaders. Teach us to submit to them just as Christ submitted to the will of the Father, giving his life as a sacrifice for us. We are yours.

Submission – Part 3

What is the opposite of peace and quiet? Chaos and noise.

What is the opposite of godliness? Godliness means living by God's law. Wickedness is its opposite. Wickedness is evil behavior.

What is the opposite of holiness? To be holy means to be set apart, designated as special, spiritual purity. The common, mundane, corrupt, impure things are the opposite of holiness.

When we contrast these phrases, it seems simple to choose which ones we'd rather have or be. So how do we live peaceful and quiet lives in all godliness and holiness? Paul gives the answer in his first letter to Timothy:

"I urge, then, first of all, that requests, prayers, intercession and thanksgiving be made for everyone - for kings and all those in authority, that we may live peaceful and quiet lives in all godliness and holiness. This is good, and pleases God our Savior" (1 Timothy 2:1-3).

Did you catch the how-to part at the beginning? We can life peaceful and quiet lives in all godliness and holiness by submissive prayer for our leaders.

Prayer (by request and by giving thanks) for everyone in authority over us leads to living a life that avoids chaos and unnecessary noise, avoids wicked and evil behavior, and frees us from the common, the mundane, the corrupt, and the impure.

Let's please God our Savior by spending time praying for the following leaders in our lives:

- Leaders of our government
- Leaders at our jobs
- Leaders at our schools
- Leaders in our church
- Leaders in our homes
- Other leaders

Lord, we pray for your blessing and favor upon our leaders. Guide them to make godly decisions. We thank you for their leadership, even when we may disagree with them. Teach us to submit to their leadership as we submit to you. Make us yours.

Submission – Part 4

Sometimes the things God asks us to do seem pleasant. Other times God asks us to do things that seem unbearable. Consider the story of a man named Jonah. He hated the ministry he was asked to perform.

"The word of the Lord came to Jonah son of Amittai: 'Go to the great city of Nineveh and preach against it, because its wickedness has come up before me.' But Jonah ran away from the Lord and headed for Tarshish. He went down to Joppa, where he found a ship bound for that port. After paying the fare, he went aboard and sailed for Tarshish to flee from the Lord. Then the Lord sent a great wind on the sea, and such a violent storm arose that the ship threatened to break up" (Jonah 1:1-4).

Jonah's stormy cruise wasn't the only negative consequence of running away from God. When the others on board found out Jonah was running from God, they threw him overboard (in the middle of the storm). If the storm was strong enough to capsize the boat, certainly Jonah didn't stand a chance of swimming to safety. Luckily (if I can say that), Jonah was swallowed by a giant fish, only to be puked up several days later - disgusting consequences for running from God!

Notice verse three: it doesn't say Jonah ran away from what God asked him *to do* (although he did). Rather, it says Jonah ran away *from God*. What do you think this means?

Scripture tells us that God arranges the parts of his body (the church) to function in the way he chooses (not in the way we might choose). By including us in his ministry, God asks us to be responsible and accountable to the leaders he has placed over us. When we "run away" from what they ask us to do, we are running away from God.

So what does "running away" from what we are asked to do in ministry look like? It shows up as arrogance, selfishness, laziness, and irresponsibility. It is evidenced by not maintaining a healthy relationship with God. It means setting a poor example or being sloppy. It will look different for each of us. But the consequences are the same: Running from God ruins ministry potential.

Lord, help us to honor, support, and follow the leaders you place over us in ministry and throughout our lives. We may be asked to do things that stretch us beyond comfort. So we will choose to submit to our leaders as we submit to you. Replace arrogance with humility, selfishness with transparency, laziness with order, and irresponsibility with accountability.

Develop our relationship with you. Use us as good examples. And improve our skill as you shape us to be the kind of worship leader this ministry needs us to be. Make us yours.

Submission – Part 5

In 2011, a major earthquake led to a catastrophic emergency at the Fukushima nuclear plant in Japan. As fears increased and problems compounded, people began to ask, "Who is in charge?!?" Sometimes this question is asked to determine who to blame when someone goes wrong.

Child after child seems to be asking the same question repeatedly. When a child doesn't like a decision made by a parent or teacher, they begin to ask, "Who is in charge?!?" Sometimes this question is asked when people want to challenge authority over them.

When a person is struck by great difficulty – health concerns, financial ruin, troubled relationships, or more – they can often overcome the fear and despair associated with their difficulties by remind themselves who is in charge. Those who trust in our God know that his plans for us are beyond the circumstances of this life. Sometimes this question is asked to instill peace and hope.

Whatever the motivation for asking who is in charge, ultimately there is no authority above our God. We read this in Colossians 1:

"He is before all things, and in him all things hold together. And he is the head of the body, the church; he is the beginning and the firstborn from among the dead, so that in *everything* he might have the supremacy" (17-18).

In what areas does our God have supremacy? In everything, it says. No exceptions. We are accountable to him. His authority cannot be challenged. And in him we find the ultimate source of peace and hope.

When we recognize the supremacy of our God, we respond in complete submission. When we are awestruck by his splendor, we are humbly reminded of our place. When we yield control to God, he invades every corner of our lives. Sin is dragged into the light and extinguished. Selfishness is replaced by compassionate love for others. Habits change. Attitudes are reshaped. Decisions alter course. And our lives reflect true worship of the One who is truly supreme.

Lord, we place you before us in all things. We cannot hold all things together; yet you do. Be the head, the leader in control of our lives and ministry. Begin a new life within us as we follow your direction in submission to your will. In everything we are, have, and do, have supremacy. Make us yours.

Submission – Part 6

Have you ever met someone who always seems to talk about themselves? Constantly trying to impress others, ensuring that everyone knows about their accomplishments, these people seem to need the approval and acceptance of those around them.

This is what Scripture calls preaching about yourself. Rather than telling people about how good our Lord is, some people spend time and energy trying to convince others to like them. This is not the attitude of a follower of Christ, a minister, or of a worship leader.

"What we preach is not ourselves, but Jesus Christ as Lord, and ourselves as your servants for Jesus' sake" (2 Corinthians 4:5).

When you spend more time acting like a servant of Christ (instead of a servant of your self-image), your ministry will become increasingly more effective, and our Lord will be greatly honored. This kind of submission means worrying less about what other people think of you, and worrying more about what other people think of your Lord. Let your attitude and behavior reflect well upon him and his reputation.

Lord, we submit our self-image to you. Make your reputation more important to us than ours. Fill our mouths with your praise, not our own. Humble us as your servants, that our lives might honor you. We are yours.

Submission – Part 7

As he prayed in the garden, Jesus knew his death was coming soon. He understood that God's plan for our salvation had a great cost - his own life. As the day approached, Jesus prayed over and over again. He had some difficult decisions to make regarding whether he would be willing to complete God's mission. Let's read about these prayers.

"Then he said to them, 'My soul is overwhelmed with sorrow to the point of death. Stay here and keep watch with me.' Going a little farther, he fell with his face to the ground and prayed, 'My

Father, if it is possible, may this cup be taken from me. Yet not as I will, but as you will.' Then he returned to his disciples and found them sleeping. 'Could you men not keep watch with me for one hour?' he asked Peter. 'Watch and pray so that you will not fall into temptation. The spirit is willing, but the body is weak.' He went away a second time and prayed, 'My Father, if it is not possible for this cup to be taken away unless I drink it, may your will be done'" (Matthew 26:38-42).

- How did Jesus describe the way he felt? (v 38)

- Did Jesus want to do what God had sent him to do? (v 39, 42)

- What steps did Jesus suggest would help guard his followers from falling into temptation? (v 41)

- What does it mean to be watchful?

- Jesus said "the spirit is willing, but the body is weak." Whose "body" do you think he meant? Whose body was in danger here? Could he have been talking about himself?

- The "cup" he talked about symbolized Jesus' role and responsibility. His job was to suffer and die. This isn't a cup that anyone would want to "drink." Would you have done it if you were him?

Jesus gave us the ultimate example of what submission looks like. Although he was scared to death ("overwhelmed with sorrow to the point of death"), he still submitted to God. Not my will, not my desires, not my plan... no, let's do it your way, God, your will, your desire, your plan. Our attitude should be the same as Jesus Christ's.

Lord, thank you for your willingness to give your life for the penalty of my sin. Thank you for submitting to the Father, even when it meant suffering and dying a wrongful death. Help us to follow your example of submission. Even when it costs us, we will do what you ask us to do. Even when it's scary, difficult, painful, or inconvenient, we will still submit to your will. Make us yours.

Final Thoughts…

Jesus told a peculiar story in Matthew 22:1-14. Take a moment to read it now (I'll wait).

Now that you've had a chance to read this parable, what do you think it means? How does it apply to worship?

I believe that our experience in congregational worship is much like getting dressed for the party. I love the lyric of the Christmas song *Silent Night*. It says,

"Fit us for heaven to live with you there."

The guy who got thrown out of the party wasn't allowed to stay because he hadn't dressed right. This isn't about clothes. It's about the preparation of our hearts, the condition of our lives, the willingness we have to join God's party – his way of doing things, his design for life.

Take your job as a worship leader seriously (whether or not you get paid). Your role in shaping the lives of those who worship is *vital*. You are helping them to get ready for the party.

So let's rock!

Measuring Your Success

The Worship Leader Assessment measures the same areas of worship leading that are addressed in this book. When all ten areas become strengths of the worship leader and worship team, their ministry is best equipped to honor God and serve his people.

What is the Worship Leader Assessment?

The Worship Leader Assessment is an online tool to measure the health and growth of worship leaders and worship teams. It involves a series of statements to which participants respond, evaluating their strengths and weaknesses in ten areas of worship leading. By understanding areas of needed growth, worship leaders and worship teams can implement strategies to take the quality of their ministry to the next level. This honors God and serves his people.

Who is the Worship Leader Assessment for?

The Worship Leader Assessment is for pastors, leaders, singers, band members, choir members – anyone who helps lead worship. Individual participants can use the Assessment to identify areas of needed growth and to track their progress over time. Worship Team Leaders can use the Assessment with their entire team (band or choir) to identify strategies for growth, encourage team members, and reflect on their personal leadership needs.

What is the process for using the Worship Leader Assessment?
The Worship Leader Assessment is designed to work in four stages.

1. In the first stage, you'll work with your worship team to complete the Team Assessment. It involves a graph that you'll print and fill out together as a team. (If you're using a single license, you can still complete this stage on your own).

2. The second stage is when individual participants will complete the online Assessment. Each participant responds to a series of statements about their worship leading habits. This stage continues until all team members have completed the online Assessment.

3. In the third stage, the team leader will have access to view your team's results and begin implementing strategies for growth. This stage varies greatly from team to team, and is customized to meet your team needs.

4. The fourth stage is optional, but highly recommended. In order to track your progress and regularly identify areas of needed growth, we recommend that worship teams take the Assessment every 6 to 12 months. Comparing results to previous Assessments is a useful means of seeing the changes that are taking place in your worship team over time.

As an owner of this book, you'll get a discount when you use The Worship Leader Assessment. To learn more about how The Worship Leader Assessment can help measure your health, suggest strategies for growth, and track your progress, visit

http://www.worshipbanddevotions.com/worship-leader-assessment/

Yours

You have probably noticed the words "We are yours" and "Make us yours" at the end of each prayer throughout this book. Our experience in congregational worship is one of the many ways God uses to make us his, to shape us into the sons and daughters he desires for us to be.

If you would like to learn new worship music written specifically about this concept – asking God to "Make us yours" – consider adding my CD entitled "Yours" to your collection of music. You can listen to samples, download sheet music, and buy a CD at

http://www.ShapingWorship.com/yours

Other books by Pastor Steve Baney

You may also have interest in these other books written by
Pastor Steve Baney.

Devotional Books…

> The Daily Devo – Volume 1
> The Daily Devo – Volume 2
> Shaping Worship – 70 Devotions For Worship Leaders and
   Teams

Discipleship Resources…

> Purpose at the Park - A Simple Four-Step Community
   Outreach Guide
> Good Friday Worship Experience – Seven Stations of
   Contemplative Worship
> Ready… Set… Seven Devotions For Short-Term Mission
   Teams

Children's Books…

> The Hopeful Worm
> Leonard Likes Lizards
> Dancing With Fishes

For more information about buying copies of these books,
please visit

http : // shop . my own little reality . com /

(no spaces)